WOMEN WRITERS IN FRANCE

Other Rutgers Books by Germaine Brée

MARCEL PROUST AND DELIVERANCE FROM TIME

AN AGE OF FICTION: THE FRENCH NOVEL FROM GIDE
TO CAMUS (with Margaret Guiton)

CAMUS

GIDE

WOMEN WRITERS IN FRANCE:

Variations on a Theme

GERMAINE BREE

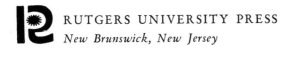

RUTGERS UNIVERSITY PRESS
New Brunswick, New Jersey

Library of Congress Cataloging in Publication Data

Brée, Germaine.
  Women writers in France.

  (The Brown and Haley lectures)
  Includes bibliographical references.
  1. Women authors—France. I. Title.
II. Series.
PQ149.B7   840'.9'9286   73–13700
ISBN 0–8135–0771–5

for Esther Wagner

CONTENTS

The 1973 Brown and Haley Lectures are the twentieth of a series that has been given annually at the University of Puget Sound, Tacoma, Washington, by a scholar distinguished for work in the Social Studies or Humanities. The purpose of these lectures is to present original analyses of some intellectual problems confronting the present age.

PREFACE

At the end of the fourteenth century in France, a woman, Christine de Pisan, took her contemporaries to task for their unenlightened attitude toward women. Although the consequent debate, known as the "querelle des femmes," is probably familiar to students of French literature, it is perhaps not common knowledge. Nevertheless, it seems a most topical subject, related as it is to one of the major cultural issues being widely debated at all levels of our society.

But as a subject of an essay, it presented some difficulties. The first but not the least of these was to avoid the monotony of an enumeration of names and works, many of which would mean little to the reader and which would result in a kind of patchwork, reductive rather than in any way illuminating. It would have been possible, perhaps, to limit the scope to our century and to a few major figures, such as Colette or Simone de Beauvoir, in an attempt to give some appraisal of their achievements against the broader background of twentieth-century literature, perhaps in relation to the more vigorous literary presence of women writers in England and the United States. But, beyond the fact that the topic seemed limitless, I felt that this approach would obscure many facets of the situation of the French woman writer and, in particular, the long and rich tradition of feminist writing reaching back to the twelfth century. The fortunes of French women writers over these centuries and their attitudes toward literature and society, the issues they raised, some of which still remain unsolved, seemed to me to offer a more fertile field for our consideration.

The choice may seem overambitious, and obviously it called for simplifications. The essay does not propose to give a systematic account of the achievement of French women writers over eight centuries or of the social context in which they wrote. Although, of late, studies on the situation of women and of women writers are beginning to accumulate, there is still a great deal more to know about their historical and social condition. What I sought to do, rather, was to place today's "querelle des femmes" in a wider perspective, to give more depth, perhaps, to our debates concerning the creative capacities of women, to add to our awareness of their presence in our literary heritage, and to throw some light on the more specifically French aspects of the case.

Actually, a more general question concerning the status of literature itself is being debated in France. It is perhaps implicit in the following statement by the anthropologist Claude Lévi-Strauss on the invention of writing, which retrospectively throws some light on my topic:

The only phenomenon which, in all parts of the world, seems to be linked with the appearance of writing . . . is the

establishment of hierarchical societies, consisting of masters
and slaves and where one part of the population is made
to work for the other part. . . . And when we consider
the first uses to which writing was put, it would seem clear
that it was connected first and foremost with power . . .
exercised by some men over other men and over worldly
possessions. . . . Therefore, the problem of progress becomes more complicated . . . for if, in order to establish
his ascendancy over nature, man had to subjugate man and
treat one section of mankind as an object, we can no longer
give a simple and unequivocal answer to the questions raised
by the concept of progress.[1]

Perhaps then it was in some measure the subordinate position
of women that allowed the brilliant literary tradition of the
West to develop. And only to the extent to which a woman
could emancipate herself from that subordination while still
maintaining her position in a "hierarchical society" could she
achieve the status of writer. Thence the ambivalence of the
woman writer's position in regard to society which seems to
recur in the patterns adumbrated in this book. If, in Sartre's
terms, writers are by definition cast in the role of the "bad
conscience" of a society, then possibly the woman's situation
has, more than the man's, been torn between respect for the
established cultural world to which she aspires and her sense of
the inequities that world imposes upon her. However that may
be, the conflict is undeniably acute today. It is perhaps the fundamental pattern that emerges in this wide-ranging glance back-
ward over the centuries.

This book consists of three lectures that were given in March, 1973, at Puget Sound University, the twentieth in the distinguished Brown and Haley series. The honor carried with it a particular burden of responsibility, for I was the first woman lecturer invited to speak in the series. I wish to take this occasion to thank all those at the University of Puget Sound, faculty, students and friends, for the cordial welcome extended me and the interest with which the lectures were received. To President R. Franklin Thompson; to Professor John Magee, Chairman of the selection committee of the Brown and Haley Lectures, and Mrs. Magee; to Professor and Mrs. Sinclair and to Professor Esther Wagner, I wish more especially to express my appreciation for the kind hospitality which I fully enjoyed. It was gratifying to note the interest that Mr. Fred Haley and the Haley family personally take in the lectures they sponsor, thus creating a rare and highly laudable bond between Town and Gown. In the preparation of this publication I have been greatly indebted to Anne L. Martin of the University of Wisconsin, whom I take this opportunity warmly to thank.

Germaine Brée

April, 1973
Madison, Wisconsin

WOMEN WRITERS IN FRANCE

"Un livre de femme, c'est un livre qui refuse de prendre à son compte ce que font les hommes. Beaucoup d'hommes n'ont jamais écrit que des livres féminins."

Jean-Paul Sartre
Situations, IX, 18–19

CHAPTER ONE

THE "QUERELLE DES FEMMES," OLD AND NEW

In 1953, Marcel Béalu, a French poet, published an *Anthology of French Feminine Poetry from 1900 to the Present*.[1] It included the names of thirty women poets, a "partial and incomplete" selection, he noted, which he had undertaken because he realized how few women were included in anthologies of poetry. Indeed, the year before, an anthology of contemporary poetry [2] listing close to three hundred writers had mentioned a dozen women poets but only four of these were represented by even a single poem.

However, for the moment I shall leave aside the question of the numerical imbalance in favor of another: the question of "feminine" poetry, of "feminine" literature in general. The problem was raised by Marcel Béalu, who questioned the poets themselves, but unfortunately quoted only two answers: "What do I care about feminine poetry, if it exists! It is probably nothing but a classification malevolently or lazily established" (p. 8). The second: "A few years ago, a young woman writer conducted a survey among her 'sisters' who wrote under a masculine pseudonym to ask why they had made that choice; the answer was often that it was a matter of prudence, the fear of critics [who are] inclined to judge 'feminine' literature unfavorably, to classify it as 'ladies' handicrafts,' " like needlework, for example. "They hoped," continued the poet, Jeanne Sandelion, "to impose themselves a priori by this apparent virility, as if a feminine pen, with few exceptions, was not immediately recognizable. I'd add that it *should* be immediately recognizable, if it brings an original and valid message" (p. 8). These two answers, simple as they seem, raise questions that are at the heart of a controversy that reaches beyond literature, which is our concern here, and yet deeply affects both the woman writer and the critic.

No one, presumably, would raise the question of "male poetry." What the first poet, Edith Boissonnas, was saying is that in the evaluation of poetry as such, sex is irrelevant; Jeanne Sandelion, in contrast, was reflecting first on the social condition of the woman poet and secondly on the inevitable link between a person and his or her work. One recalls Virginia Woolf: "It would be a thousand pities if women wrote like men or lived like men," she wrote in *A Room of One's Own*, "for if the two sexes are quite inadequate considering the vastness and variety of the world, how should we manage with one only?" [3] The dilemma of the critic dealing with "feminist" literature is posed. Terminology here is of some importance and in itself points to the cultural dimensions of the question. The term "feminine" carries with it connotations clearly enshrined in Webster: "tender, soft," as opposed to "robust, strong, male." And although "feminist" quite properly designates only "a feminine expression," it has acquired a militant color. Whereas "male," Webster informs us, besides referring to sex, denotes "an intensity or superiority of the characteristic qualities of anything," "female," we are informed, "applies to animals and plants as well as human beings and always suggests sex." Although one may, like Edith Boissonnas, abhor the fact that in matters of literature a qualifier is necessary, I have chosen throughout to use the term "feminist literature" as referring merely to literature written by women.[4]

It may at first seem strange that the question should come up at all in France in the mid-twentieth century. For France is a country that has prided itself on a long tradition of successful women writers dating back at least eight hundred years. There was Marie de France in the twelfth century, about whom we know little; in the fifteenth, Christine de Pisan; then the brilliant group of noble ladies of the Renaissance; in the seventeenth, Madame de Sévigné and Madame de Lafayette; the great hostesses, memorialists and letter-writers of the eighteenth; Madame de Staël and George Sand in the nineteenth. In the twentieth century, in a Paris that has harbored Colette and Gertrude Stein, Anaïs Nin, Katherine Mansfield, Simone de Beauvoir, Nathalie Sarraute and Marguerite Duras—to mention only a few of a throng of distinguished women of letters—one could hardly remain unaware of the increasing number of books being written by women or of their quality. Yet the number of women writers who still use pseudonyms, though relatively lower than at the turn of the century, is still high, raising the question of the status of the woman writer which Marcel Béalu's apologetic anthology emphasized. Is feminist literature still considered and evaluated as a particular kind of literature, not on a par with "literature" as such, a by-product secondary in its significance? Is there such a thing as a recognizable "femininity" that with some exceptions has confined the woman writer to minor accomplishments in that realm? Do successful women writers show different characteristics from their male counterparts?

In our mid-century years it was a woman writer—and a successful woman writer—Simone de Beauvoir, who, in her monumental treatise *The Second Sex*, published in 1949, arose in wrath to destroy the current notions of femininity; we know with what bitterness and eloquence she denounced signs of male resentment and superciliousness in the manner in which French male critics evaluated her own books. She connected this trait with the much broader question of the image of women held—overtly or covertly —by French society and thus launched anew in France the ageless and unresolved debate concerning women with which we have lately become all too familiar. The initial "querelle des femmes" took place at the dawn of the fifteenth century, 1398–1402, and has gone on, more or less heatedly, ever since, surfacing in times of social unrest—during and after the French Revolution, for example, and again in our time.

Today's widespread "querelle des femmes" took on a specific coloring in the atmosphere of Paris, of French society, of the existentialist perspective in which it was formulated. It has been vigorous; some of the major exchanges at the higher level of intellectual debate being *An Open Letter to Women* by Francis Jeanson, a philosopher and friend of Simone de Beauvoir's, who disagreed with some of the latter's points; an eloquent, virulent answer, *An Open Letter to Men,* by Françoise Parturier, another friend of Simone de Beauvoir's, a distinguished woman journalist and minor novelist; and finally, a restatement of the question from a different perspective, *The Misunderstanding of the Second Sex,* by Suzanne Lilar, a woman lawyer, playwright, and essayist, who starts with a thorough critique of Beauvoir's thesis and goes on to propose one of her own.[5] These are only a very few of the innumerable essays, long or short, thoughtful or passionate, that the debate has inspired, either in special issues of current reviews or under such titles as *Tomorrow Women, Woman in Search of Herself, Liberated Woman?* I shall not recapitulate the arguments; we listen to them here every day.

On another level, French sociologists have been exploring the status and, more interestingly for us, the "image" of woman in the different strata of French society.[6] Their conclusions, far more objective in tone than the controversies engaged in by the literary milieu, throw an interesting light on the debate. The status of women in France has changed, slowly since the mid-nineteenth century, but quite rapidly since World War II. But until quite recently, and fairly consistently in all classes of French society, the *image* of woman, the manner of representing her, has not greatly evolved. Since 1946, French women have obtained civic rights and increasingly have won equality—theoretically, and to a certain degree in practice; but only now is the full impact of the change upon French society beginning to appear. If, as the sociologists point out, the liberation of women entails a change in the entire network of social relations, of value systems, it affects the equilibrium of the whole society, and what they call the *images-guides* or "guiding images" of the culture lose their validity. Thence a rift between fact and attitude, the violence and confusion in the debate concerning them.

How does this relate to my topic? It obliges me, first, to examine the question of the manner in which women writers have been evaluated in French histories of literature: are the issues raised by Madame de Beauvoir concerning the attitude of her critics valid? And how about the literary historians? How have they approached feminist literature? In an attempt to answer these important questions, let us take as an example a single book, which in a sense volunteers itself, a book which came out in the twen-

ties, entitled *History of Feminine Literature in France* by
a certain Jean Larnac,[7] one of the staples in the field. He
opens with a moving statement of objectivity, but nevertheless with a thesis: "I should like to show [in this book]
the continuity of the literary effort of women and to
reveal in their works what is specifically feminine and
makes a whole that is very different from masculine literature" (p. 5), it being understood that women's writings
are "foreign to the masterpieces of masculine genres." He
seems to posit, simply, that feminine art is of a different
form. It was Larnac's purpose, he notes, to counter Joseph
de Maistre's answer to his daughters who, in the early
nineteenth century, had petitioned their father to allow
them to study literature with their brothers. Women, their
father answered, had written no masterpieces in any genre:
"they composed neither the *Iliad* nor the *Aeneid*, nor
Phèdre nor *Tartuffe*—etc."; consequently, he had refused
their request. This is the insidious accusation raised in
regard to all the arts, which, for painters at least, Linda
Nochlin answered in a vigorous and well-documented
article in *Art News* entitled "Why Are There No Women
Painters?"[8]

Let us look at Larnac's approach. For example, when he
is dealing with the beautiful Louise Labé, the lyrical Renaissance poet, whom he admires: "To classify her would be a
useless effort. . . . That is because she wrote according to
her heart, her flesh, her senses, her nerves. Her poems seem
to be the spontaneous fruit of genius" (p. 68). And then

comes Marie de Gournay, Montaigne's adopted daughter: "an ugly old spinster who had claimed to be only a brain." He compares the two women: "the former [Louise Labé], turning on all her feminine charms, the second seeing salvation only in masculinization. The public chose between the two methods: Louise Labé was celebrated as a goddess; Marie de Gournay was laughed at *à l'envi*" (pp. 68–69). This is a rather strange way to assess literature—basing one's judgment on the erotic attractiveness of the author. Besides, what Larnac says is not true: in her day, Marie de Gournay was a highly esteemed and successful woman.

Mr. Larnac's attitude recalls that of Gustave Lanson, the authoritative historian of French literature, concerning another, earlier woman writer. Lanson dismissed the late medieval author Christine de Pisan as "the insufferable bluestocking whose indefatigable facility was evenly matched by her universal mediocrity"; [9] she who, to her contemporaries, was Dame Christine with the "golden pen" and whose works were translated into English by order of Henri VII:

> Of these sayings Christine was authoress
> Which in making had such intelligence
> That thereof, she was miror and maitresse . . .
> Her work testifie the experience. [10]

And, in 1971, in a literary history of the Middle Ages, she is again honored as one of five major "creative" figures of the period between 1300 and 1480.[11] Neither for Christine de Pisan nor Marie de Gournay were contemporaries grudging in their praise. These two women, who earned their living by their pen, France's first professional women writers, were, in fact, in spite of the difficulties they encountered on the way, financial and literary successes. But let us take up Larnac again and turn to two well-established women writers of the Classical period, Madame de Lafayette and Madame de Sévigné. Madame de Lafayette, who with *La Princesse de Clèves* developed a new kind of novel, was disappointed in love, Larnac notes. "Was she so ugly? Yes, if we judge by the portraits we have of her; no, according to the Duke of Retz, who was a connoisseur in the matter. I think nonetheless that she must have had more inner charm than real beauty, which would explain her early disappointment. . . . Whatever the case . . . she abandoned the fight for love and attempted to become famous by a means other than beauty—talent" (p. 121).

Madame de Sévigné, at least, was not ugly. But "would she have desired fame if she had married someone other than the Marquis de Sévigné—unfaithful, agreeable to women, detestable to his own? One may doubt it. . . . In her case, the love of fame replaced love itself. It was a value of replacement. . . . And I wonder if these substitutions of which the seventeenth century shows us many examples did not bring more or less hidden regrets? Who knows if Madame de Lafayette, seeking happiness in fame

after having vainly sought it in love, was not sorry she
had thus oriented her life?" (p. 106).

Well now, surely the celebrated Madame de Staël, a
century and a half later, was not deprived of love; yet
"Would she have oriented her life in the same way if she
had possessed the beauty of Madame Récamier? I think
not. . . . She lacked a specifically feminine charm. . . .
To obtain the happiness love refused her, she resolved to
conquer fame, which was only for her, according to her
famous words, "le pis-aller du bonheur," a poor substitute
for happiness" (p. 175). What characterizes her as a
writer, besides the obvious defect to which our compas-
sionate critic attributes her desire to write—an unwomanly
lack of charm (where men, of course, have genius)—is
"her incapacity to reach outside herself" (p. 181). "Whatever one may say, she did not have a creative mind. . . .
As for the ideas which have been much emphasized, she
did not invent them: she borrowed them from those
around her" (p. 181). Just like Madame de Lafayette:
"*She* owed to her friends the outline [of her novel], the
historical documentation, all that her lack of imagination
did not allow her to put together, she owed to them
the perfection of her style. . . . What remains [is] the
intimate life . . . of her novel—the first novel in which
a human heart is dissected" (p. 126). One understands
Beauvoir's exasperated, excessive, and defensive reaction
against male myths in *The Second Sex*.

It is a fact that French literary historians have been

particularly slow in shedding the often ironically indulgent "eternal feminine" approach to feminist literature. How deeply they have affected women's own idea of what they should be writing is still an open question. Mr. Larnac's definition of a woman writer's realm is simple and clear: he has as his model for the woman writer a woman poet of the Romantic era, Marceline Desbordes-Valmore—as he sees her, of course. "No woman writer showed less intelligence; none, in contrast, showed so much sensibility. No [correct] spelling in her manuscripts. Did she know what assonance was? Alliteration? No invention, no creative imagination, only complete truth of the heart. . . . Love was the foundation of her life" (pp. 197–201). We are fairly warned: it is not feminine to deal with ideas or to excel intellectually.

We are not surprised when, in his conclusion, this obscure paragon of intelligence traces the "limits" of the feminine "genius," making a few illuminating remarks, on the way, that have a bearing on the general question of the reputation of women writers. He is concerned with the acclamation won by such women writers as Delphine Gay, an immensely successful playwright, novelist and journalist, also of the Romantic era: "her beauty created the illusion [that she was great]. One doesn't forgive a bluestocking, even if she has talent—witness Marie de Gournay. One approves everything, in contrast, in a pretty woman. . . . For thirty years Delphine Gay made lovers of her readers and spectators. As soon as she disappeared,

enthusiasm was deflated" (p. 216). Or again, speaking of
the debate concerning women's intellectual capacity that
followed in the wake of the Revolution, Larnac notes that
Proudhon "brought a little common sense to a subject that
passion had obscured." Having examined meticulously the
intellectual possibilities of "women," Proudhon, he reminds
us, reached the following conclusion: "From the point of
view of intelligence, she has perceptions, memory, imagination. What is lacking: the capacity to produce seeds, that
is to say, ideas, what the Latins called genius" (p. 189).
That kind of common sense is familiar; it is exactly the
one which our historian himself posited in his book from
the start. The equation: instinct = woman, intelligence =
man, is a widespread cliché even today. When instinct is
prized over reason, then the woman writer will benefit.
When not, as in Mr. Larnac's case (for in his eyes the male
"genius" of rational thought is an inherent component
of great literature), she suffers. In consequence the scale
of values proposed limits a priori the potential of the
woman writer and the range of critical evaluation applied
to her work.

I need not push this any further; and Mr. Larnac no
doubt is an easy target. But his idea of the suitable feminine
realm in the arts, though simple, is not unique: naïveté; a
song arising from the heart; a single theme, love; writing as
a *pis-aller;* and the incapacity of women to deal with ideas.
What, if any, idea of women writers does one get from
such a book? None; only an idea of "woman"—an arche-

typal woman—emerges from its pages. Most certainly few critics would now so openly advertise such conceptual smugness, linked to such naïveté concerning the nature of literary expression.

But the close connection of the feminine image with the critics' evaluation of the work women have achieved is illuminating. And most damning is the image of the woman writer as one who takes to the pen when she "fails" in her role as a woman: too ugly and thereby unloved; and who is, as it were, redeemed from her disgrace only when she "expresses" her emotions directly, emotions centered, of course, upon a man. Until lately this conception has been far more widespread in shaping literary criticism and even feminist works than is generally admitted. Certainly many solid studies on French women writers have been written by men. But the resurgence of the "querelle des femmes" today induces us to rethink French literary history, to look anew at the role of women writers in its development. One positive result of the new "querelle des femmes" has been the rediscovery of many hitherto forgotten women writers, often by women scholars, and the development of a new perspective on some women writers summarily dismissed in the past. I shall first turn briefly to the original late medieval and Renaissance "querelle des femmes" for the light it may throw on our own more recent one. Second, I shall examine the women writers' position and accomplishments in the pre- and post-World War II periods as typified by two very

different figures, Colette and Simone de Beauvoir. Finally,
I shall look at the picture today in an attempt to see how
most profitably the question of the woman writer may
be stated.

A list of names of women writers would mean as little
as a historical survey. But I think a quick look at a cluster
of early French women writers—significant figures in the
realm of letters, whom I call the "initiators"—may prove
fruitful in spite of the distant social and cultural milieu
and the intervention of from four to two hundred years.
Of these women, Christine de Pisan (1364–1430?) is the
first. Born in the fourteenth century, she preceded the
other three of whom I shall speak by a hundred and twenty
to two hundred years. But she is, in every respect, their
precursor; and in some respects she is the first modern
French woman we know. She moved to France from Italy
when she was three years old, for her father, Thomas, who
was a doctor and an astrologer, was sent as an envoy from
the Doge of Venice to the court of Charles V, whose
councilor he subsequently became. A man of learning as
well as wealth, Thomas saw to it that the daughter, of
whom he was very fond, could read and write, besides
French, Latin and her native Italian. At fifteen, he chose
for her among her suitors "the one who had the most
knowledge with *bonnes moeurs*," good character. The
marriage was a most happy one, as witnesses one of her

ballads, "Douce chose est, que mariage (A Sweet Thing
Is Marriage)," and as she tells us in yet another poem:

> His company was
> So pleasing to me when he was
> Close by! There was never a woman alive
> More contented with her lot.[12]

But in 1380, the fortune of the family began to change:
her father's patron and protector, King Charles V, died;
the Dauphin was a sickly boy who, when he became King,
was given to spells of insanity. In a France where, during
those waning years of the century, the feudal system was
fast disintegrating, the rivalries between such powerful
and ambitious figures as the King's uncles—the Duke of
Orléans and the Duke of Burgundy, who eventually made
an alliance with the English—plunged France into a new
phase of the Hundred Years' War; and anarchy reigned
until such time as a young girl, Joan, took it upon herself
to lead the French armies to victory and the Dauphin of
France to his coronation at Rheims.

The death of Charles V spelled ruin for Christine's
father, who soon followed his king to the grave. Ten years
after her marriage, when she was twenty-five, Christine's
husband died of the plague, leaving her with three small
children to care for. It was then that she began to write,
in the deep distress of that loss.

Today, a month ago,
My dear one left me.
My heart is sad and numb
Today, a month ago.

(P. 33)

She later recalled her plight: "When he was in the flower of his age, competent and ready, as much in knowledge as in wise and prudent ascendancy and control, about to rise to high positions, Fortune took him from me in the flower of his age, when he was thirty-three years old and I was twenty-five. And I remained alone with the charge of three small children and a large household" (p. 35). Alone and facing ruin, with no protectors, cheated and harassed by unscrupulous dealers, "desiring more to die than live," she nonetheless took up the fight. "And you may understand that for me, a woman weak in body and naturally fearful, it was hard work to make of necessity a virtue" (p. 37). It was then that she started to earn her living by the pen, acquiring a modest economic independence that guaranteed her a personal freedom rare for a woman in those days.

Against the backdrop of war, court life at the time revolved around Queen Isabeau. It was turning in upon itself and reviving the courtly modes of the past, the themes and decor of *l'amour courtois*. Writers in those years sought patronage at court. Literature was a highly conventional affair and the task of writers was ritually to celebrate their patrons and the events of court life in the intricately patterned verse forms of the day. It was a fellow poet, Eustache Deschamps, who taught Christine the rules of the game: "I started to forge pretty things," she writes. And so that her son would have a proper education, she also started to study:

> Son, I have no treasure
> To enrich you!
> For treasure, I now
> Shall note for you
> Some teachings.
>
> (P. 49)

Christine took to learning with passion:

> . . . for I am fated
> To occupy my life [with learning]
> And I'll never wish
> To leave that path.
>
> (P. 57)

And so began her extraordinary career as a "scholar among women." She produced fifteen volumes of work contained in seventy large notebooks. Her writings became increasingly broad in scope, as she undertook the vast, objective treatises on politics, on the art of government, on peace, that won her a comparison with Boethius. Rambling and overdocumented with erudite quotations and allusions

though they may seem to us, to her contemporaries they
seemed modern and learned.

Her first success came when she launched the controversy concerning women. Her target was the famous
Roman de la rose, a long poem in two parts: the first is a
compendium of the rules of courtly love; the second, by
an antifeminist cleric, Jean de Meung, is an exposition of
the traditional medieval attacks on the misdeeds of Eve.
It was one of the most widely read books of the time, a
typical literary exercise showing two traditional, contra-
dictory and equally mythical male images of woman, the
courtly and the clerical. As scholars have suggested, it is
probably because Christine had a direct experience of
what the nature of the relations between men and women
really was outside the closed circle of courtly ritual—that
is, brutal and demeaning for women—that she undertook
to challenge those relations in a long poem, *Epistle to the
God of Love.* She attacked male attitudes to women in no
uncertain terms and from the point of view of her own
experience. What did a woman encounter in her dealings
with men? Lack of respect, extortion, defamation, betrayal.
As far as she was concerned, the *Roman de la rose* and
Ovid too (another favorite book of the time, and in her
eyes a manual on how to deceive women) were fit only
for burning. She thought, of course, within the conceptual
framework of her time concerning the hierarchy of the
sexes, drawn from the familiar story of the Creation and
the Fall.[13] So she based her arguments upon the wide gap

between the image of man in his role as representative of
God's reason and order and the realities of his conduct;
and between Jean de Meung's antifeminist description of
women and the women she observed, herself among them.
In other words, she held up to men a far more realistic
image of themselves and their failure to live up to their
role and blamed them for misrepresenting women in their
books. She suggested too that, had women written those
books, a different light would have been thrown on the
subject.

It would be tedious to recapitulate the arguments
aligned, but Christine's was a passionate and yet sensible
defense that won for her the protection of the Queen,
and, more significantly, the friendship of a powerful and
enlightened ecclesiastic, John Gerson, the Chancellor of
the University of Paris. Gerson was aware that the times
were changing and that the old codes of behavior were
disintegrating; and he seems to have appreciated the basic
rationality of Christine's approach. Daniel Poirion, a
medieval scholar, sees in the conjunction of the two
figures, Christine and Gerson, the first signs of a totally
new social configuration, announcing the humanistic and
rational Renaissance.

"For the first time in France," writes Poirion of Christine, "the story of a literary work cannot be separated
from the study of a personality. Here is . . . our first
author, and that author is a woman. And because she is
a woman, [as a writer] she avoids many shortcomings of

the period." [14] One of these being, of course, the gratuitous
pedantry of the age. In her case, he notes, one feels that
the expression and the feeling coincide exactly; speaking
for herself, she spoke for all women. "I took as example
myself and my way of living, as a natural [normal]
woman, and in the same way also the other women I
frequented, princesses, noble ladies, ladies of middle or
low condition, who, most kindly, told me their private
and secret thoughts." Christine was committed to the
defense of "toute l'université des femmes," present and
to come.

It is pleasing to note that after some years of silence in
a retirement caused by the violence of the civil wars,
Christine took up her pen again, alone among the writers
of her time, to celebrate Joan of Arc, when the rumors
of the Maid's exploits reached her in 1429, as "the honor
of the feminine sex":

> A sixteen year old girl . . .
> For whom arms are not too heavy
> It seems in fact that she thrives
> On them, so strong and hardy is she
> And before her, her enemies are in flight.[15]

It did not surprise her at all that God had chosen a woman
to save the country; to those who pointed out that the
Church had condemned Joan, she answered: "What Dame
Joan has done was well done, and by the commandment
of God."

I shall recall, more briefly, three women writers of the Renaissance. The first is Marguerite d'Angoulême (1553–1615), later Queen of Navarre. She was the sister of Francis I, to whose career she devoted her energies. A woman active in politics who shared the Renaissance passion for knowledge, she started out better equipped than Christine, for she was thoroughly well-grounded in the major classical and medieval texts that formed the corpus of knowledge at that period, and she was familiar besides with Dante and Petrarch. She gathered in her entourage some of the best minds of the time. During the Renaissance, learning enjoyed an unrivaled prestige in court circles, and Marguerite was one of the many women of the high nobility who mastered that learning. Like Christine, she wrote prolifically, in a great variety of forms in both verse and prose: dialogues, *oraisons*, spiritual meditations, plays, a spiritual autobiography, and finally, the famous unfinished collection of sometimes ribald short stories in the tradition of Boccaccio, the *Heptameron*. In her handling of the traditional *conte*, she modified its intent and structures, giving it a new depth and significance. She was a studious and deeply meditative woman with a broad and often trying experience of life in a society where highborn women were pawns in a political power game. In the humanistic learning of the time she sought a personal understanding of life and of the Christian religion. Underlying her work is her personal spiritual odyssey. She was drawn to the new philosophical trends,

the Neoplatonism which was to bring about a reassessment
of the doctrines of the Church. Like Christine, she too
appears as an innovator: "Beyond the fact that philosophical and religious poetry in France goes back to
Marguerite, that she is the first mystical poet in our
literature, we owe her something more precious and greater
still: a scrupulous attention, honest and unswerving, to the
movements of consciousness, the appearance of the 'moi'
[the self], in literature." [16]

The contrast could hardly be greater than with Louise
Labé (1524?–1565?), a generation younger, and certainly
no Neoplatonist. Celebrated in her time as the "French
Sappho"—a term we shall encounter again in one form
or another—she produced only one small volume of purely
lyrical love poetry and a *Debate of Love and Folly*, a
dialogue in five parts, highly original in form, which
today's critics are looking at with renewed interest. She
lived in the city of Lyons, then in its heyday as the second
capital of France, called the "French Florence." It was
at the time the city of printers, close in spirit to the free
and brilliant way of life of Renaissance Italy. Louise Labé
was the daughter and later the wife of wealthy merchants,
ropemakers—thence her name, *la Belle Cordière*. Her
father idolized his daughter and saw to it that she got a
first-rate education: in Greek, Latin, Spanish, Italian. She
knew Dante, Boccaccio, and Petrarch, and learned the art
of music; she later had a fine collection of books in her

library. She rode horseback in male attire and jousted like her brothers. She married late for the time, at twenty-five, a man thirty years her senior, who seems to have left her the greatest freedom. This was a time of small circles or clubs of men and women enamored of the new culture. In Louise's circle there were many celebrated poets, both male and female, precursors of the better-known Pléiade group: Ronsard, Du Bellay, Rémy Belleau, etc. Her house and garden became the gathering place of a brilliant and talented circle of friends, who practiced the Renaissance art of civilized living, cultivating poetry, music, friendship, and love until the Wars of Religion plunged the city into disaster and ruin. Clément Marot, the protégé of Marguerite de Navarre, was one of her circle, as was Amadis Jamyn. The inner circle of the "Lyonnais" poets comprised such figures as Maurice Scève and another gifted woman poet, Pernette du Guillet. Louise sought no protectors and needed none, for she was an independent woman. It was to a friend, Mademoiselle Clemence de Bourges, that she dedicated her slim volume of love poems, justifying their publication:

Since the time has come, Mademoiselle, that the severe laws of men no longer prevent women from applying themselves to sciences and disciplines, it seems to me that those who have that facility should employ that worthy freedom which our sex desired so greatly in the past to study these and to show men the wrong they did us by depriving us of the good and the honor which these [studies] could bring us; and if one of us should reach such a level as to be able to put down her conceptions in writing, she should do it carefully and not disdain fame and make of it an adornment rather than [adorn herself] with chains, rings, and sumptuous clothes, which we can only really count as ours through the use we make of them.[17]

Though not made to command, women, she felt, should be the companions as much in "domestic as in public affairs, of those who govern and are obeyed" (p. 12). She points to the good that comes from writing as one who has experienced it. Pleasures and feelings pass instantly, she notes, "but when it happens that we have put our conceptions into writing, even though our brain afterwards pursues an infinity of affairs and moves incessantly, taking up what we wrote a long time later, we come back to the same point and the same disposition in which we then were" (p. 15). And this, she adds, gives "a singular pleasure." Clearly the experience is a personal one, and it is expressed in the limpid, musical language that characterizes her poems. The feeling seems strangely modern that makes of writing the vehicle of "time regained"! For a long time it was the woman Louise and her love-life that fascinated critics, moved by the passion and sensuousness of her poems; what astounds us today is rather her originality, her unique mastery of the poetic idiom she developed, almost untouched by the current mannerisms of the day.

For the last of these exemplary women, I admit I have a personal sympathy: Marie de Gournay, the "French Minerva," who was to become Montaigne's spiritual daughter, a relationship that was recognized in their day. Born in 1566, at a time when the Wars of Religion were about to plunge France once again into chaos (there were eight wars between 1552 and 1598), she was the eldest of six children and seems to have been a particular favorite of her father, who died when she was eleven. In order to survive, the family retired to the provinces, where this extraordinary young woman taught herself how to read and learned Latin "without the help of any Grammar," together with some Greek, while stubbornly refusing to get married. In 1584, when she was eighteen, she fell upon a book that had just come out, the *Essays* of Montaigne. It came as an illumination. Happily for her, since her family had begun to think she was mad, Justus Lipsius, "the most erudite man in Europe," proclaimed the then-obscure *Essays* to be a great book. On the strength of this corroboration, Marie de Gournay persuaded her mother to take her to Paris, where she wrote to Montaigne, asking to see him. He called on her, fascinated, he said, by the judgment she had made of his essays: "She a woman and living in these times and so young and alone in her province . . . a circumstance worthy of high consideration." [18] He was to entrust to her the editing of his work after his death. In the meantime, like Christine, she had become head of the family, a family in debt; like Christine, she decided to live by her pen, and concurrently fulfilled her task as head of the family nobly. For herself, she adopted a way of life that was truly new. She resolved to "have no other husband than her honor enriched by the reading of good books." She took a house in Paris; then, when money became scarce, she moved into a small apartment with a companion and a cat, and, besides devoting much time to the defense and promotion of Montaigne, wrote mightily and fought mightily too in the battles of the day, some of which concerned the intellectual capacity of women. She produced a novel, treatises on education, language and poetry, and a defense of her own way of life: she was a deeply committed woman of great integrity. She was also a perspicacious critic and a magnificent satirist. And she won out. Attacked and lampooned by some, she became nonetheless a highly respected figure in Parisian society; her salon was frequented by the most active and interesting men of letters of the time; indeed, it was from that salon, it has been suggested, that the idea of the French Academy was launched. She lived, active and honored, to the age of eighty.

I have sketched these portraits briefly; they should suffice to kill once and for all any stereotyped image of the feminist writer, so diverse are they: scholar, philosopher, poet, critic. Yet all these women do have certain things in common: the fight they put up in favor of the emancipation of women, of "honneste liberté"; and the manner in which they themselves lived their own freedom. All four could have signed Marie de Gournay's treatise on the *Egalité des hommes et des femmes* (*Equality of Men and Women*) and her *Grief des dames* (*Complaint of Ladies*). (Some of these "griefs" are taken up again in Parturier's *Open Letter to Men,* more particularly the exasperating complacency of rather stupid men who refuse to listen to women who are more intelligent and better informed than they are.) All four claimed for women the right to an education and refused to accept current opinions on the natural inferiority of a woman's mind. One could quote endlessly from what they wrote on the topic. Even the apparently most uncommitted of them, the poet Louise Labé, exhorted women to raise their minds above distaff and spindle; to learn for "their own contentment and to show they could surpass men in that realm."

One can detect certain similarities in the social situation of these women that may explain their careers: three of them belonged to an aristocracy that in itself freed them from certain forms of social constraint; it was the flowering of a liberal spirit in the bourgeois society to which she belonged, coupled with her wealth, which gave the fourth, Louise Labé, her independence. The women benefited from the great prestige of learning in the circles in which they moved; all four were passionately drawn to books and because of special circumstances had access to

them. Because they *were* women, they had not been shaped
in the scholastic mold. It was perhaps because of their
very position as "outsiders," not admitted to institutions
of learning, that, in a time of rapid social change they were
able to some extent to detect more clearly than most of
their male contemporaries some of the essential trends and
social myths of the moment.

They lived at a time when a form of culture and with
it a way of life were drawing to an end, and by their own
independence and integrity, in their sphere, they broke
away in small measure from obsolete constraints. They
flourished within small, select circles of men and women
where a certain decorum prevailed between the sexes that
counteracted or masked the injustice of the condition
against which they rebelled. They all seemed to have felt
the need for the sustenance of feminine friends and found
comfort in feminine examples of achievement. It would
seem, at least for three of them, that an initiation into
learning through the interest of an indulgent father was
an important factor in their development.

There was, however, no dominant male figure in their
adult lives to impose upon them a certain way of living.
All four moved freely beyond the narrow limit their
society ascribed to feminine life; and all four enjoyed the
friendship and respect of eminent men, who were in touch
with the new concerns, knowledge, and ideological trends
of the time. They seem to have had one great advantage
as writers: for them, writing was never a game, a pas-

time, or an erudite display, gratuitous, of knowledge. It was rather a means to self-knowledge and perhaps self-affirmation; thence their originality. That originality too perhaps explains why their quality as writers eluded not so much their contemporaries but later scholars intent on generalizing and cataloguing. They astonished their contemporaries, not because of their "feminine" qualities, but because they thought and wrote as well as the best of men.

CHAPTER TWO

THE DIVIDED IMAGE:
SEDUCTIONS AND REDUCTIONS

Notwithstanding the experience of centuries, which has proved that woman is, without exception, incapable of any true artistic or scientific work, female doctors and politicians are being forced upon us in the present day. The attempt is useless, since we have not yet produced the female artist or musician, notwithstanding all the desperate efforts of the daughters of concierges and of all the marriageable young ladies in general who study the piano, and even composition, with a perseverance worthy of greater success; or who make a mess with oils or water-colors; who copy from plaster models or even from the nude, without being able to paint anything but fans, flowers, plates or very indifferent portraits. . . . Woman on earth has two parts to play, quite distinct roles—but both of them charming—Love and Maternity. . . . To woman in fact, it has been given to dominate and enchant man merely by the form of her body, her smile, and the power of her glance.[1]

So, with the force of conviction if not of logic, wrote Guy de Maupassant at the end of the nineteenth century,

33

in a preface to a famous eighteenth-century novel by
l'Abbé Prévost, *Manon Lescaut*. Echoing across almost
three centuries, one can almost hear Marie de Gournay's
exasperated reply:

> And if women reach degrees of excellence less often than
> men, it is a wonder that the lack of a good education, in
> fact, the abundance of the professed and bad one has not
> done worse, preventing them from getting anywhere at all.
> Is there more difference between men and them [women],
> than between them [women] and themselves, according to
> the kind of education they have had, whether they were
> brought up in cities or villages, or according to their nation?
> And why would not an education equal to that of men in
> the affairs of the world or [the realm of] letters fill the
> void which generally appears between their heads and the
> heads of these same men? [2]

Over the intervening centuries the same battle of words
had continued, but women in the upper classes in France
had made considerable social, if not legal, headway. In
spite of the support the influence of Cartesianism brought
them, their slow path to emancipation was strewn with
the old arguments, however glaringly the facts belied those
arguments. Our imaginary Maupassant-Gournay dialogue
summarizes sketchily but vividly the two sorts of emancipation offered, though Maupassant obviously did not fully
realize the implications of his statement. *Manon* is the
tale of an eighteenth-century courtesan who chooses to

use her charm not as a "wife and mother," but to obtain full sexual freedom, the right to her own way of life. It was not the kind of choice that Marie de Gournay had envisaged; *her* choices to withstand the social conventions did not involve that kind of freedom; *she* believed in the supremacy of intellect and rationality.

These two attitudes converged in the figure of Ninon de Lenclos (1620–1705), the woman who, in the seventeenth century, won from French society her right to conduct herself sexually according to the rules applied to men without forfeiting her rank in society. Brilliant, renowned in all Europe for her great intelligence, she was surrounded by a few women of talent and many distinguished men. She was proverbially straightforward in her dealings with men; in her liaisons she followed her whims but never lied to her partners or unduly exploited them. She was, like the *fin de siècle* society she frequented, skeptical and rational, unruffled by the nature of the relations that allowed her a reasonable financial independence; demystifying their sexual aspect in favor of friendship. "Every night I give thanks to God for my mind," she is said to have remarked. "Every morning I thank him for preserving me from the follies of my heart." The impeccably respectable Marie de Gournay or Christine de Pisan would not have recognized that, choosing as she did the independence of the single life, she was in a way their child. She is one of the women Simone de Beauvoir admires. She notes:

The Frenchwoman whose independence seems to us most like that of a man is perhaps Ninon de Lenclos, seventeenth-century woman of wit and beauty. Paradoxically, those women who exploit their femininity to the limit create for themselves a situation almost equivalent to that of a man; beginning with that sex which gives them over to males as objects, they come to be subjects. Not only do they make their own living like men, but they exist in a circle that is almost exclusively masculine; free in behavior and conversation, they can attain—like Ninon de Lenclos—to the rarest intellectual liberty.[3]

If by rejecting the double standard, Ninon de Lenclos won intellectual freedom and equality with men, she did not, with the exception of a satiric comedy and a few letters, put it to literary use. She was to a certain extent the model of a long line of women who, whether in or out of marriage, lived with considerable freedom outside the set patterns of society, creating their own intellectual environment, sought after because their salons combined, in varying degree, urbanity, freedom, and, for men, a path to success—political, social, or literary. For the women of the Renaissance, learning was a fulfillment in itself. But because of its prestige in that society, it was also for them a form of power, a path to a personal dignity and recognition within their circle, of a kind different from the social dignity they enjoyed as members of a dominant class; writing, with the intellectual discipline it required, could raise them to a position of companionship with eminent men, in equality and mutual respect. For Ninon, however, the achievement of the social art of living freely, intelligently, on an equal footing with intelligent men, was sufficient in itself. This image of the sophisticated, brilliant, emancipated woman largely countermanded the more austere images of the women writers who were her contemporaries, such as Madame de Sévigné (1626–1696) or Madame de Lafayette (1634–1692). Madame de Sévigné made of letter-writing an art, a literary genre, but her letters went unpublished in her time, and Madame de Lafayette, a novelist, long concealed that she wrote at all.[4] Both lived independently but discreetly,[5] and they developed their skill as writers within and for a small, select circle of friends. Within that protective circle, both fashioned out of current forms of writing—the letter and the novel—a new literary style. Like Louise Labé, they were purely literary artists, but they were situated more centrally at the core of a cultural movement, in closer contact with an elite aware of the new aesthetic requirements of the hour. Beside them, another type of woman writer appeared, a type which became legion, exemplified by the celebrated Madeleine de Scudéry (1607–1701), their senior by a quarter of a century, who lived well into her ninety-fifth year, surviving them both. She was one of the high priestesses of an aristocratic group, the *précieuses*, who rose in revolt against the coarseness of manners and language that had prevailed since the end of the Wars of Religion and that underscored the basic brutality of the relationship

between the sexes. To counter this they strove to reinter-
pret the courtly codes and manners of the past, adapting
the more gallant aspects of the Italian Renaissance to a
society which once again was settling down to urban life
in Paris. Writing at first under the protection of her
brother's name, Madeleine de Scudéry, better known to
her contemporaries as the "illustrious Sappho," poured out
indefatigably and with enormous success an endless flow
of novels that epitomized the new code of manners and
sketched, under transparent masks, the somewhat embel-
lished personalities of her readers. It is a matter of note and
perhaps should be a matter for study that, in the footsteps
of Madeleine de Scudéry, women novelists in France have
unflaggingly produced the most popular "period novels,"
usually written with deftness, if not high distinction.

The society which glorified Ninon and the *précieuses*
while at the same time harboring Sévigné and Lafayette, an
increasingly permissive one, was scheduled to disappear
with the Revolution. It had favored the emergence of a
large number of remarkable women—and of some frivo-
lous and impossible ones—but these were women for whom
learning was a social grace and no longer a burning passion; women who excelled in conversation, in letter-
writing, in such personal genres as memoirs, fairy-tales
and popular novels; women who belonged to an elite, who
lived at the hub of the social and literary establishment,
but as spectators or patrons rather than as actual participants. This is the role the salons maintained when the

Revolution swept over France at the end of the eighteenth century, and with it they consummated a divorce from the main trends that shaped French literature in the next century. "In republics," Montesquieu had noted in 1748, "women are free by law; slaves by custom." [6] He was contrasting the lot of women under republics with that of women under monarchies, whose rituals, being largely dependent upon the presence of women at court, indirectly gave women scope, in the labyrinths of court politics, for the exercise of their powers of seduction and hence of power itself. But Montesquieu had not foreseen what could happen to women in republics where they were tied down by law and ambivalently considered by custom. The French Revolution stirred French women deeply, both those of the bourgeoisie and women of the people. Feminist clubs sprang up, and active feminist demonstrations claimed the right of women to participate in full citizenship. Powerful male voices spoke in their favor, among them the Marquis de Condorcet's, whose words recall Marie de Gournay's: "Custom may familiarize mankind with the violation of their natural rights to such an extent that even among those [women] who have lost or been deprived of those rights, no one thinks of reclaiming them or is even conscious that they have suffered any injustice." [7] He refutes the tenacious notion of the superiority of the male mind, "which is not the necessary result of a difference of education." But the bourgeois image of woman proved stronger than Condorcet's reason; the clubs were closed, a few women leaders guillotined (like Condorcet himself) ; and it was Napoleon Bonaparte who defined the French woman's civil status for more than a century—well into the twentieth. Napoleon's view of women is well known; it is enshrined in the *Code Civil* and reiterated in his *Mémorial de Sainte-Hélène:* "Woman's role is not self-realization but to serve." "Woman is given to man so that she will have children. She is therefore his property, in the same way as the fruit tree is the gardener's." In this new society in the making at the dawn of the industrial age, the Napoleonic code tied the French woman firmly down to the family, making her in every manner a minor, economically and legally dependent on man; and a stigma was attached by that society to the woman who did not conform. Thus at the time when the Romantic image of the alienated artist was also arising, the difficulty for women was compounded; literary and social circles no longer reinforced one another in the same way. This conjunction affected the woman writer's position adversely: social respectability and literature parted company.

It was outside of the Paris salons that the two dominant women writers of the nineteenth century made their careers. The Revolution and Napoleon's antipathy threw Madame de Staël (1776–1817), that great disseminator of ideas, into the broader frame of Europe and an itinerant life; and the stanch, provincial, bourgeois[8] George Sand (1804–1876), the most successful of the mid-nineteenth-century French novelists, lived the life of an *honnête homme* à la Ninon, outside accepted social circles. A professional writer, journalist, and purveyor of *feuilletons,* she earned her living and recognition in the turmoil of the literary market place through hard work. Both Staël and Sand, like their eighteenth-century predecessors, transcended and denounced the limitations imposed by their society upon a woman's life. Again, in their case, this concern was part of a larger one, a concern with the movement of history: for Madame de Staël it took the form of an acute sense of new intellectual horizons opening in the modern world, and it led George Sand to become involved in the social movements that mark the epoch.

But at the end of the nineteenth century, the *fin de siècle* salons, on the whole, whatever their averred political positions, and although they "received" famous writers, had become, like the French Academy itself, conservative, aesthetically divorced from the vital creative forces of literature. "Salon-culture" had little of the solidity it had had in previous centuries. A bevy of women novelists and poets belonging to salon society were writing; some, like the poet Anna de Noailles (1876–1933), enjoyed tremendous success; we find most of them largely unreadable today. Perhaps under closer critical scrutiny, either psychoanalytical or sociological in kind, their works might yield a number of themes and patterns that would go a long way towards defining these women's real, as opposed to their official, image of themselves and perhaps the source of their weakness. No one has depicted better than Marcel Proust the society in which this early twentieth-century wave of feminist writing manifested itself. And to some extent it both condones and explains, though it does not excuse, belated Romantic attitudes toward women such as Mr. Larnac's.

In the first decade of this century, which Roger Shattuck has called the Banquet Years,[9] "Paris-France," Gertrude Stein noted, was the city where the art of the twentieth century was being forged in music, painting, sculpture, and, more slowly, in literature. But it was not being forged in the salons, nor, really, through the established reviews, the literary prizes, or the proclaimed literary celebrities of the hour, Anatole France, Maurice Barrès, and Pierre Loti. Once again a *fin de siècle* Paris society had become established, where the *grande bourgeoisie,* the aristocracy, the glamorous "sacred monsters," actors and actresses (Sarah Bernhardt and the Duse), mingled freely. It was a lavish society in which the elegant, the beautiful woman was queen, a society that never tired of the spectacles it provided for itself, of itself, in its infinite leisure. Women reigned officially in sophisticated Paris circles, women cast in the glamorous role of *objets d'art.* But their position was in fact not conducive to achievement in any real sense. The most celebrated women of the Romantic era, Marceline Valmore and Delphine Gay de Girardin (a woman, as Larnac, you may recall, reminds us, celebrated for her beauty), had both belonged to nonbourgeois, specialized milieux—theater and journalism—where a woman, with an enlightened husband, had access to the world of literary publication controlled by men. But women in general were in fact irresponsible children before the law. The Romantics, following Rousseau, had provided the concomitant myth: women, mysterious, ethereal, were made for love and death, a myth Flaubert's heroine Emma Bovary tried to live, in fact, and for which she was cruelly punished by her creator.

The movement of liberation had continued slowly, but rather through social action than through literature. At the beginning of the twentieth century, approximately when Maupassant was recording his disapproval of the trend, the first women's lycées had been functioning for some twenty years (since 1881) and women had begun to appear in many professions: the first doctors, the first lawyers, journalists, directors of reviews; dozens of women novelists and poets were writing. But the Romantic mystique was still prevalent, the image of the "instinctive woman," of the passionate woman untrammelled by learning, who sang as she felt, a woman whose narrow realm was passion and the search for sensuous fulfillment and for whom writing was "feminine" self-expression. The feminine heart and the feminine senses were her domain, and her genius was a matter of temperament.

When we read the most celebrated woman poet of the period, Anna de Noailles, from our present viewpoint, we are confronted and dismayed by the sustained outpouring of a rich rhetorical language cast in an outdated verse form. In poem after poem, Anna de Noailles pours out her sense of herself as reflected in "nature," a nature that reflects back to her in turn only her own fervent infatuation with her image of herself as an inspired woman poet. In a self-indulgent society she is without doubt, and most unfortunately for her own talent, a kind of unadulterated Narcissus, living in her own closed world. She offers us a typical image of a feminine writer and feminine writing. It is true too that we are only now beginning more carefully to scrutinize the many women poets who achieved some celebrity in those years. More carefully—more favorably too; perhaps a changed attitude will bring about a changed evaluation of their work. Some of the best among these women writers of the early twentieth century withdrew into a feminine world, a world of rather claustrophobic and self-conscious lesbianism, as if, in answer to a society that relegated women to marginal roles as writers, wanting to be writers, they had to deny masculinity, as an assertion of feminine autonomy. No one was to know femininity and describe it better than Colette, who in *The Pure and the Impure* (1932) evoked the tragic and pitiful fate of one of the most talented of these women, the poet Renée Vivien (1877–1909).

Meanwhile, in the realm of the now-forgotten and overabundant novel, Maupassant's alternate chiding and praise of women was taken up again and again. Novelists unstintingly warn women—especially the innocent *jeunes filles*—of the unfortunate results any further emancipation would have for them. They constitute a rather comic chorus in which men and women participate equally, with such books as *Blue-Stocking, Emancipated Women, The Evasion, The Liberated Woman, The Virile Virgins, The Rebel* (in French, the title, *La Rebelle,* is feminine), *Princesses of Science* (one recalls that Marie Curie had at last been permitted to give a university course a year before *that* novel came out), *The Ladies of the Law Courts, In the Garden of Feminism,* to quote only a few titles. Others take up the age-old arguments in their favor. "It seems to me," wrote a woman novelist, journalist and critic of the fifties "that the woman writer of 1900 . . . never stopped looking furtively across at the man, comparing herself to him, measuring up, opposing him, trying finally to seduce him through the prestige of an intelligence or a sensuality that at last dared express itself. To the woman who said 'I want to vote too. In any case, I've read Plato,' another answered 'I've got a sex too; you shall know my desires.' " [10] And she attributes to this hesitation and indirectness the fact that women writers lagged behind out of the literary mainstream: "They missed out on surrealism, missed out on the broad movement toward the social novel before 1914, missed out on the [postwar] *malaise du siècle,* its adolescent evasions and anxieties" (p. 63). But so too, we should add, did many male novelists; though less amateurish, their novels have also slipped into oblivion.

It is a fact that the great majority of women writers in

the *fin de siècle* and pre-First World War years lived un-
seeingly in the world that produced a major revolution
in aesthetics. Whether society women or bourgeois women
active in the literary circles and established literary rituals
of Paris, they were, like many of their male counterparts,
unaware of what was taking place around them. They
were marginal beings in a class of society on the way out,
engaged in marginal literary activities; their main occupation often consisted in maintaining intact the glamorous
round of social life, with its patterns, taboos, and hier-
archies. The contrast is obvious with the solid figure of a
Gertrude Stein or, a little later and more modestly, of a
Sylvia Beach, discovering Joyce; or an Adrienne Monnier
receiving in her bookshop near the Odéon the significant
"new writers" of France, of whatever class. In the twenties,
after the upheaval of war, a new type of woman writer
appeared, often university-trained, conscious of her intellectual powers, less willing to accept either her relegation
to the ranks of feminist writer or the current definition of
her feminine nature.

In this context, the person and the work of two women
are particularly striking; both achieved wide fame, reaching far beyond the boundaries of France. One was Colette
(1873–1954), who came to Paris from her province in
1893 with her totally corrupt and not-so-charming fifty-
year-old husband, Willy, to live and thrive as a writer in
its most dissolute—some would say decadent—circles;
Colette, twice divorced and thrice-married, whose love

affairs often echoed scandalously in the social chronicles of a press that loved scandal. But she steadily plied her craft as a writer, working single-mindedly at her writing through all vicissitudes; and in the end, rather heavy though she had become and crippled with arthritis, she reached, as indisputably as any movie star and more durably, a quasi-mythical stature in the eyes not merely of the literati, but of the people of Paris. And, younger by a generation, was Simone de Beauvoir (b. 1908), who started her career as a student of philosophy in Paris a quarter of a century later than Colette, entering into a life-long pact of friendship with, but maintaining her independent status from, one Jean-Paul Sartre. It is interesting to note in *The Second Sex* Beauvoir's unstinting admiration for and praise of Colette, from whose writings she draws frequent examples to corroborate her analyses. Toward the end of her book she assesses Colette's achievement. She had previously spoken of the deleterious effect on women writers of the requirement, so carefully cultivated by French society, that women please; and, in contrast, she evokes Colette:

> It is not because of her gifts and her temperament alone that Colette became a great writer; her pen has often been her means of support, and she has had to have from it the same good work that an artisan expects from his tools. Between *Claudine* [allusion to the title of Colette's first series of tales] and *La Naissance du jour* [*Break of Day*], the amateur became a professional, and that transition brilliantly demonstrates the benefits of a severe period of

training. . . . We admire in Colette a spontaneity that is not met with in any male writer. . . [but] it is a well-considered [carefully studied] spontaneity.[11]

For Claudine Chonez, Colette's writing is "as it were, the hinge, the transition between the old feminist literature and the literature [now produced by women] which is slowly imposing itself." [12] And she names the successors of Colette, the harbingers of that new literature: Simone de Beauvoir, Simone Weil (1909–1943), Marguerite Yourcenar (b. 1903). All are indeed women of considerable stature, who have at least one thing in common: a rigorous training in philosophy. Colette's formal education, in contrast, stopped approximately at the level of our junior high school.

No one was more clearly aware than Colette herself of the shortcomings and uncertainties that marked the writing of her feminine contemporaries and of their source in feminine attitudes themselves. No writer, male or female, has ever probed more deeply, observed more dispassionately nor more lucidly described a conflict she herself experienced as a young woman, between her stubborn addiction to writing and her needs and role as a woman in regard to her male partner. No writer has ever probed as deeply nor more dispassionately described what she calls the Inexorable, that is, the power of the senses, concentrated in sexuality to mold and dominate the human animal. *The Pure and the Impure* in this respect marks an epoch in

French literature. It is a lucid, absolutely honest personal meditation by a woman on the exigencies and modes of sensual desire and satisfaction in men and women, heterosexual and homosexual. In the course of the meditation, Colette examined her own dilemma, both as she confronted the covert sexual hostility of men to a woman whom they considered in some respect "virile," and as she experienced her own conflicting exigencies: the dispassionate objectivity and independence of the writer, the sensuous submission and physical-biological dependency of the woman. She was fifty when in *Break of Day* she called for a truce in what she sees as the inevitable sexual joust:

> Come, Man, my friend, let us simply exist side by side! I have always liked your company. Just now you're looking at me so gently. What you see emerging from a confused heap of feminine cast-offs, still weighed down like a woman by seaweed (for even if my head is saved, I cannot be sure that my struggling body will be) is your sister, your comrade: a woman who is escaping from the age when she is a woman. She has, like you, a rather thick neck, bodily strength that becomes less graceful as it weakens, and that authority which shows you that you can no longer make her despair or only dispassionately. Let us remain together: you no longer have any reasons now for saying goodbye to me for ever.
>
> Love, one of the great commonplaces of existence, is slowly leaving mine. The maternal instinct is another great commonplace. Once we've left these behind, we find that

all the rest is gay and varied and that there is plenty of it. But one doesn't leave all that behind when or as one pleases.[13]

In the perspective and vocabulary of the day, untouched as yet by Freud, she saw herself as an intellectual and biological androgyne: male because of her commitment to her writing, female in her body and being. This conflict between the "woman's role" as understood by French society and that of the writer is clearly stated by Colette. Through her meditation on her own dilemma, she throws considerable light on that of other women, like Renée Vivien, whom she observed closely.

"From my post, behind a desk-table. . . my woman's eyes followed, on the turquoise velum, a stubby and hardened gardener's hand, writing." Writing! Sixty titles, seven thousand pages bound in twelve large volumes, writing extending over half a century, some of it occasional writing, since, off and on, Colette earned her living as a journalist—one of her side-ventures, along with the music hall and a short-lived commerce of beauty products. Her best-known works are a half-dozen short novels or stories: *Gigi* (1944), more particularly since its film version; and the two unclassifiable works written in the twenties, *La Maison de Claudine* (1922) (*My Mother's House*), and *Sido* (1929). And it is indeed in the twenties and thirties, when she was in her fifties and sixties, that Colette produced the works that established her, along with Proust, Gide, Valéry, and Claudel as one of the great writers of her age.

Not that she resembled them. At a time of great literary sophistication, when literature had entered a phase of self-questioning and aesthetic renewal, Colette propounded no theory, no ideology. In some respects, the substance of her work recalls the *fin de siècle* motifs of her contemporaries and thereby puts off a critic like Henri Peyre, who sees in it only "boudoirs and bedrooms, aging roués, courtesans and brainless gigolos," devoid of heart, whose "introspective life is so elementary." [14] The motifs—but not the perspective; for two factors rescued Colette from the feminine *fin de siècle* narcissism, its false ingenuousness and equally artificial sophistication. The first was her provincial childhood and the presence in her life of the mother whom she celebrated under the name of Sido; the second, Willy, the man who locked up the twenty-year-old girl and obliged her to write, her cicerone in the dubious cuisine of commercialized literature (he had a literary "stable" of hired hack-writers whose work he signed, and he used Colette as one of them), the agent too of her initiation into "those pleasures we so lightly call physical."

Colette had been, she never forgot, "a dearly loved child of parents who were not rich and lived in the country among trees and books," one of four who lived in freedom under the protection of Sido, a woman closely attuned to the rhythm of plant and animal life, whose bidding to the children was "look"—look at the wasp, at the spider, at the iris bud unfurling, at the light in the sky; a woman who loved and protected all living things, which she accepted unsentimentally in their beauty, strangeness, and ferocity. Under Sido's tutelage, in the garden of her childhood, Colette developed an exceptional acuity of perception and precision in observation; thence her ability to restore freshness and mystery to the commonplace. Left to herself, she felt not the slightest need to write. It was Willy who forced her to begin and who suggested the material, her own experience, embellishing her first accounts with *fin de siècle* perversities. The compulsion to write was thus born, and it was sustained by financial need, but when Colette divorced her husband it became a self-imposed duty and a discipline. Stage by stage, Colette learned her craft as a writer: "I have been writing for fifty-three years. For fifty-three years the concern for my material existence and deadlines have imposed their rhythm upon my life. . . . I don't know when I'll succeed in not writing." [15] She wrote with an exigent critical sense always on the alert, in stubborn opposition to the myth of a necessary feminine abandon in expression.

Where most of her male admirers have stressed the "miracle" of her writing, its "naturalness," and proclaimed that it was a gift precluding analysis, she always stressed the underlying labor. And she found her own domain from which she would not be deterred: "I believe," she wrote of one of her men friends, he wanted to "expand (I would have said 'restrict') the scope of my life by the help of some great idea. . . . Out of malice, and to get my own back, I asked him one day whether he could conceive of what a

life laid waste by a single idea would be like." [16] But if
Colette refused abstraction, she developed a personal perspective in the long meditations that sustained her relation
with what she observed. Her domain as an artist is the
drama of what she called the "Inexorable," the imperious
life of the senses that govern human, like animal, needs and
desires. Of these, the rituals of sex are the most revealing;
the attractions and repulsions, the avidity, the inevitable
polarization and conflict which bind into a couple two
beings who, she noted, are not necessarily seeking each
other's well-being, but who are as they are, and as such
must live out their assigned roles as biologically prescribed.
And she spoke of other things bodies impose and which
must be lived with—growing old, for example.

No literary personality could be further removed from
Colette than Simone de Beauvoir, no cicerone further removed from Willy than Jean-Paul Sartre, no mother less
like Sido than Simone's conformist one. There could hardly
be a more striking contrast between the scope and literary
quality of their works. Beauvoir's ethical, intellectual and
sociopolitical preoccupations have not the faintest echo in
Colette's, while Colette's animals, gardens, humans, and
environment belong to another planet. Though it is a fact
that "the history of literature provides no evidence of any
clear and unequivocal criteria by which we can differentiate
between the vision or style of men or women writers," [17]
one could hardly attribute Colette's work to a man. On
the whole, nothing either in subject matter or style could

be a priori marked as "feminine" in Beauvoir's. Colette's lucid and meditative acceptance of life with its servitudes and inequalities contrasts with Simone de Beauvoir's fierce denunciation of and revolt against them. Curiously enough, if one wanted to pick two figures who most typically illustrated the dominant mood of those two contrasting periods of French culture, one could hardly find two better examples. And indeed, Beauvoir does consider herself a representative figure and on the whole has thought of her work as a document of our times.

"The artist," wrote Simone de Beauvoir in one of her essays, *Pyrrhus et Cinéas,* "cannot be indifferent to the situation of men around him. In the other his very self is engaged." [18] The year was 1944, and, though the war was not finished, Paris had been liberated. In her thirty-fifth year, Simone was in "la force de l'âge," the prime of life; she was a leftist intellectual with a first novel published, and before her, an enterprise shared with Sartre and a small circle of distinguished friends, a new review to be launched, *Les Temps modernes.* In the close to thirty years since those days, Beauvoir has published five novels, a play, a book of short stories, four volumes of memoirs, three volumes of essays, two bulky sociological studies—*The Second Sex* and *Old Age*—and travel books on America and Communist China. A critic, novelist, essayist, reporter, and polemicist, she has become a leading figure in the women's struggle for equal rights and against the repressive laws dealing with abortion. And she has become a world figure, whose travels in China,

India, South America, and the United States Colette, riveted to France, would not have dreamed of.

Beauvoir's concern for mankind in 1944 was new in her system of values, for in the thirties, as she has told us in the first volume of her memoirs, her daily passion and concern had been the achievement of her own personal happiness and emancipation from her bourgeois milieu. A brilliant young woman who achieved academic distinction with ease, her personal bid for fulfillment began when she withstood her bourgeois destiny and her family's urging and refused to marry. But the years of war and occupation changed her outlook. With the Liberation, there was, she and Sartre felt, a world to be rebuilt and she, along with Sartre, thought it the duty of literature to play a significant role in that rebuilding. She had been writing since her adolescence, determined to become a great writer; but it was under the impact of Jean-Paul Sartre's ideas and in her collaboration with him that she developed her idea of the role a writer should play in a society which, she felt at the time, must inexorably move toward greater social justice via socialism. Doubly, then, she was committed to the battle for freedom: as a woman and as an adherent to Sartre's doctrine of political commitment, spelled out in his manifesto *What Is Literature?* Increasingly over the years, Beauvoir's literary work has been overshadowed by her fidelity to her political concerns in a postwar world which, since the fifties, has baffled prediction. In a sense, her novel *The Mandarins* (1954) was the postmortem of

an age, just as the four volumes of her autobiography
(1958–1972) are its partial chronicle. It is probably as a
polemicist, moralist, and intellectual who sharply chal-
lenged comfortable French attitudes toward social reality
rather than as a literary figure that she has made her mark
in our century. Her favorite models—Colette and Ninon
de Lenclos—notwithstanding, she is closer to being the
Madame de Staël or the George Eliot of our age, though a
less gifted novelist than Eliot. She is the most famous of a
group of women writers whose intellectual vigor and integrity have made it impossible to consider their work
under the catch-all title of "feminine writing," a label
Colette had transcended through the quality of her literary
craftsmanship.

CHAPTER THREE

THE UNCERTAIN PRESENT

"Simone de Beauvoir is one of the most significant writers of the twentieth century and one of the most popular writers of her generation in France and abroad. Her significance and her popularity are intimately related." [1] Elaine Marks attributes this popularity to the presence in Beauvoir's work of an obsession and unresolved conflict central to modern sensibility: a metaphysical sense of *l'absurdité*, the "emptiness at the heart of all things," and the consequent need to fill that emptiness through commitment of some kind, whether sociopolitical or directed toward art. She analyzes the impact of these conflicting attitudes and visions upon the texture of Beauvoir's writing, as Beauvoir oscillates between the moral, didactic and humorless themes of commitment to leftist ideology and the more lyrical theme of existentialist anguish in the face of death. Reluctantly, as she tells us in the last pages of the third volume of her memoirs, Beauvoir abandoned the bold stance of the forties, the belief that she as a writer had a mission; but she nevertheless continued to write, "all thought of mandate, mission, salvation gone, not knowing for whom [she] was writing any longer" (III, 679). Unlike Sartre, she seems to have turned inward, thereby again reflecting the mood of an era. "I think that literature enjoys the advantage of being able to surpass all other modes of communication, allowing us to communicate in what separates us. . . . When I read a book, a book that matters to me, someone speaks to me; the author is part of his book; literature only begins at that moment, the moment when I hear a singular voice." [2]

With the end of the Korean War, in spite of the trauma of decolonization, particularly in Algeria, a reorganized economy was rapidly moving France into a new era of prosperity. The fifties proved to be a turning-point, literary as well as political. A new generation of avant-garde writers—both novelists and critics—turned away from existential themes by "disengaging" literature from the sociopolitical preoccupations of the thirties and forties. A major shift in literary consciousness was taking place, a questioning of literary forms themselves and the assumptions upon which they rested. The "new" French writers, as they came to be called, raised two fundamental questions. One concerned the relationship between established literary patterns and socially accepted, inherited ways of seeing or constructing reality. The other concerned the phenomenon of writing itself, of how language works, of why and how a writer writes, how he deals with his heritage, that omnipresent language, "insidious, incessant and which always seems to be there before we think about it!" as Philippe Sollers, one of the "new new" writers, put it.

These questions are related to some of the major issues raised by linguists and anthropologists, who have pointed out that it is through language that men constitute meaning and order, speech being in essence a cultural activity which, for a group, takes on the aspect of a natural configuration. Men constitute their own beliefs through linguistic patterns, which in turn reconstitute their creators, so to speak. This trend favored a radical critique of the "myths" embedded in the language, a most favorable factor for the feminist cause; but it was disruptive for writers who had taken that language for granted. The writer's activity and the status of literature itself in the new technological society became crucial questions, critically examined by women writers as well as men. At the time when the breakdown of traditional social structures worked in favor of women, writing itself, its techniques and privileged position in French culture, became problematic. For some women writers, the problems of writing superseded concern over their status as women writers. In the dialogue that opposed "new" writers to traditional ones, women were divided along the same lines as men. In the realm of literature, the first generation of new writers of the fifties turned their critical attention to the novel and more to the formal conventions upon which the novel rested than actually to its linguistic make-up. Novelists, they claimed, were still working according to the patterns established by Balzac, which they endlessly replicated. The new novelists' purpose was to break or "deconstruct" the pattern, to experiment with new forms. This was really the only bond between a group of writers who have been much discussed, for each of them selected the means whereby that double task of deconstruction and experimentation was to be performed. Besides Robbe-Grillet, Michel Butor, and Claude Simon, the best-known of these novelists, the group was comprised of a number of women writers. But none has as yet attained the stature of two women writers who were associated with the "new" novel from its very beginning in the fifties, Nathalie Sarraute and Marguerite Duras. And no two writers, again, could be more different.

Born in 1903 in Russia, Sarraute was brought to France at the age of two by her divorced mother, who wrote novels; she was shuttled back and forth between France and Russia. From the French lycée she went on to the Sorbonne and a *licence*[3] in English literature, thence to Oxford to study history and to Berlin to study sociology, then returning to Paris and the law school, where she met and at twenty-two married Raymond Sarraute, who has helped and sustained her ever since. She had felt all along, she has often said, a certain desire to write; and she had read, whether in Russian, German, English or French, the novelists who have in fact created the "modern tradition" —Dostoyevsky, Mann, Proust and Gide; she was more particularly drawn to Virginia Woolf and Ivy Compton Burnett.

She struggled for many years with the difficult question of how to go about setting up the kind of novel she vaguely envisaged. She felt the need to extend and change the substance of the novel, so that it would convey adequately what she wanted to convey: a certain unexplored dimension of human psychic reality, which she sensed and experienced and which was not present in the novels she knew. Hers was a slow process of discovery, and recognition of her work came slowly; nevertheless, she anticipated by a dozen years or so the new directions which the novel eventually took. A first book of short sketches was published in 1939; subsequently, in spite of Sartre's support, her next two novels, in 1946 and 1953, passed virtually unnoticed. That is why, she once told me,[4] she wrote out of a kind of despair, the four essays of *The Age of Suspicion*, published in 1956. And at last, after twenty-five years of quasi-silence, she caught the attention of the critics. The "suspicion" of the title is neither political nor moral; it is rather the suspicion of the reader confronting a text. According to Sarraute, the novel reader of today is sophisticated and can detect all the devices a novelist uses to create the falsely plausible illusion that his fictions coincide with reality. It was in fact her own critical approach to the novels she had read that led her to explore new modes of story-telling.

She is not a prolific writer: six novels, the brief sketches of *Tropismes* (1939), a couple of short plays and radio scripts; the essays of *The Age of Suspicion,* and an article or two. She has also given many interviews, beautifully lucid, explaining how her work evolved from book to book, and she has spoken on many of our campuses with great success. Essentially, Sarraute has focused her attention on what she terms "tropisms." These are the complex inner movements that underlie, she senses, the most ordinary human contacts, beneath the surface of casual, everyday exchange. Every encounter with others, as she sees it, however banal, sets in motion a whirl of psychological uncertainty and conflict, attractions, repulsions, pleasure, fright, anger, advances, withdrawals; this under-surface world is the world of tropisms, and it extends from each to each in a common, continuously moving magma of invisible exchange or "subconversations."

This view of our psychic reality does away, naturally, with the solid character and structured plot and raises problems of technique. Since the world of tropisms is preverbal, pre-"stream of consciousness," yet continuous, Sarraute had to seek a new manner of dealing with it. She first narrowed the focus of her experiment to situations involving only two or three individuals, as she developed the technique of how to translate these underlying sub-conversations into language. Her problem was a real one, since she wanted to convey, through language, what is barely felt, never verbalized, fleeting, never arrested, impersonal, common to all, developing at different levels of awareness. Work by work, Nathalie discarded the trappings of punctuation, dialogue, or recognized narrative viewpoint. She did away with names, descriptions of landscape or social milieu; and little by little, she left out all kinds of indications, such as quotation marks, that signal to the reader what is actually said, silenced, or left unworded. It is up to the reader to follow the developing, multilayered pattern from within. To the writer's task, which is to explore and convey this new area, responds the reader's, which is to create a new manner of reading. Her texts are in fact linguistic mimes; rhythms, sounds, images modulate the vibrations that stir in the strange underlying magma, making its presence visible to the reader.

It was almost inevitable that as she progressed she should become more and more involved in the question of the literary work itself. In *Fruits of Gold* (1963) she follows the eddies caused by the appearance of a book in the literary circles of Paris; she evokes the inner and outer pressures attendant upon its writing in *Between Life and Death* (1968). Her latest work, *Do You Hear Them?* (1972), explores the whirl of tropisms set in motion in an older man's relation to his children by a shared encounter with an art object. A friend comes to dinner, and together the adults reverently examine the privileged object, a pre-Colombian sculpture; the children, after politely acquiescing, retire upstairs in a spate of giggles, to the father's inner discomfort. The book sets up one single main modulation from its beginning to its end, so that it is hard to convey the manner in which Sarraute handles language; but this is a small sample of how it develops:

> Now the laughter has ceased. After all they had to go to bed. You can't keep on babbling all night long ... and about what? Is it possible to imagine such piffle, such empty twaddle ... But it's finished, they have separated, each one has shut the door of his room, they have finally stopped talking ... there's nothing more ... and the air would seem to have grown lighter, there's a sensation of release, of freedom, of unconcern ... now he stretches out his hand and lays it on the rough stone ... It's true, it has a kind of denseness ... I'm glad that you too ... there are people who think ... And there it is starting up again ... softly ... in light outbursts...[5]

Sarraute is obliquely raising a larger question concerning a contemporary social reality in France, the counterculture and the generation gap. Her basic theme is the uncertainty of the older generation regarding its cherished values.

Sarraute is a writer of great subtlety and penetration, who blends irony and humor in a personal mode; she is unpretentious and tenacious, kindly, in a detached and observant way. Her work, though narrow in its social context, is doubly original in its technique and in its psychological premises. She does away with the individual-versus-society patterns, positing a common psychic "medium," a kind of environment, like the sea or the air, which connects all human beings at a preconscious level. Thence the fascination it exercises in an era whose tendency is to reject the dichotomy of individual and society in favor of a reintegration of group and individual. Sarraute's work has been highly consistent and deliberate; Marguerite Duras' comes free of all theory in a manner which is profoundly original and which has involved a continuous experimentation with form. Born in 1914 in Indo-China, Marguerite Duras, after the death of her father, lived the precarious life of the *petit colon*, which she described in *Barrage Against the Pacific* (1950), an early Hemingway-type novel, almost entirely autobiographical. When she was about eighteen she came to Paris, where she earned her living while studying law and political science; but some of her best writing has been haunted by the strange beauty and horror of the East, its land, its human population, and their misery. One of her strangest books, *The Vice-Consul* (1966), has as its underlying motif the song of a young, unmarried Cambodian girl, pregnant and so cast out, who wanders homeless among beggars and lepers across Cambodia and into India. Unrelated to the other characters, she and her song are a kind of thematic embodiment of the unbearable yet endured misery of the Orient. The wanderings and misery of the errant girl offer a kind of counterpoint to the adventures of a European Vice-Consul in Lahore for whom the sight, day after day, of that native suffering becomes so intolerable that at long last he shoots a gun blindly at

the lepers and dogs outside his walls, a mad gesture of
revolt against the overwhelming evidence of human pain.
His misery and that of the girl, whom he never meets,
contrast with the slick, empty life of the European diplo-
mats at the embassy. The novel is thematically constructed
more like a musical composition than a fictional narrative,
offering no analyses nor explanations.

Duras had been writing since childhood, but it was not
until 1944, when she was thirty, that she published her
first novel. Since then her work has branched out in many
directions: fifteen short novellas—or we might best call
them prose narratives—the last entitled *Love*. Her work
has become increasingly strange and hard to read, but it
obsesses and fascinates those readers who have once entered
Duras' world. She has written a book of short stories, two
volumes of plays, and film scenarios, of which the best-
known is *Hiroshima mon amour* (1960), the film for
which she wrote her first script. Lately, fascinated by the
medium, Duras has started to produce her own films.
There is a kind of fluidity or plasticity in her writing
that allows a narrative to become a play or scenario;
indeed, her works sometimes go through the three media—
narrative, play, script. Technically, Duras' narratives have
tended toward musical forms, modulating basic themes
that occur hauntingly throughout her work: madness,
suffering, solitude, but also love. Her prose narratives set
up highly stylized, simple scenarios in which characters,
identified only by name, embody the buried unconscious

needs and frustrations that, in Duras' view, haunt modern lives, blocked by the orderly mechanical patterns of bourgeois existence. Because they embody these emotional needs and deprivations, they enter into strange dialogues, encounters, and relationships. But whatever the characters and scenario, underlying them all is the theme of love— love as a mode of perception and total dispossession of the self, a love that includes the sexual as *one* of its modalities, but which does not exclude different modalities breaking with bourgeois patterns of exclusivity. Behind this idiosyncratic work stands a woman, open, direct, generous, politically passionate in all causes that involve social oppression. A communist for some years, she is now fervently opposed to the policies of the Party, a *gauchiste* who espoused the causes of the student movement in America and France with characteristic warmth. But her work is her real passion, the most important thing for her, and she is perhaps the most talented and original of writers in France today.

The later development of this literary movement of the fifties has caused a kind of basic disarray among French writers, although this is not the place to discuss the movement as it is now developing, either its often abstruse theoretical arguments or the soundness of its assumptions. But it is of interest to note among its more brilliant theoreticians two young women, Kristeva and Cixous, who are actively involved with the two most articulate and aggressive theoretical reviews, *Tel Quel* and *Poétique*.

It is perhaps a sign of the times that one naturally refers to them as one does to men, by surname alone. Basic to their approach is the sense that to write is essentially to rewrite; the written language or "discourse" is there, with its infinite number of temporary structures, continually modified in a constant interplay. This network of texts, not the writer, is the source of the literary work. The attitude, then, basically modifies the notion of "genius" so often used to destroy the feminist argument. But it also makes writing problematic. Although Beauvoir, Sarraute, and Duras belong to the same generation and have shared the same political preoccupations and often participated in the same causes, neither Sarraute nor Duras believes in a literature oriented toward political or social ends. Neither has spoken of herself as a *woman* writer; thus it is as writers rather than as women that women today confront the question of writing.

"The generation of Madame de Beauvoir was the last in France to suffer from the complex of femininity. Since then women accept themselves entirely. It gives them self-assurance." [6] Only a very young woman, one feels, could make so brave a statement. Yet it is true that in France today women writers of competence have appeared in all sections of literature: essay, novel, poetry, theater, criticism; and in fact, beyond the purely literary media, they are competently active in other forms of expression, including the movies, radio, and television. Literary Paris is no longer a male preserve; women own theaters and direct theatrical productions (Le Théâtre du Soleil, one of the experimental groups that recently has made theater history is directed by a young woman, Ariane Mnouchkine). They own and direct literary reviews; review books in magazines, on radio and television, and take an active part in all the facets of publishing and the book trade. And they write—mainly novels and essays, but also, though to a lesser extent, poetry, memoirs, or forms of autobiography. Without any question, they write as competently as the bulk of their confreres, and they have participated in the main literary and philosophical debates.

Furthermore, they come from all sectors of society: Albertine Sarrazin, whose novel, *The Astragal* (1965), was published here by the Grove Press, had served several prison terms; Violette Leduc (1907–1972) nourished her writing with the substance of her own rebellious life as an illegitimate child from a working-class milieu, an outcast, an androgyne, a black marketeer. *La Bâtarde* (*The Illegitimate Child*, 1965), her slightly fictionalized autobiography prefaced by Simone de Beauvoir, brought her a somewhat belated recognition. Christiane Rochefort (b. 1917), who shocked her reading public and opened her way to the best-seller lists by her unabashedly sexual *Le Repos du guerrier* (1958), comes from the working-class background she depicted from within in *Les Petits Enfants du siècle* (1961; translated as *Josyane and the Welfare*).

This influx of writers from the working classes has

had its consequences: a frankness in substance and language which the French women writers of bourgeois origin had tended to avoid. Marguerite Duras' parents came from a *petit bourgeois* milieu; and the *bourgeoisie,* as was to be expected, has furnished the main contingent, with, among others, Nathalie Sarraute, Françoise Sagan, Françoise Mallet-Joris, and Célia Bertin. Simone de Beauvoir has described the petty provincial aristocracy against which she rebelled. Marguerite Yourcenar (b. 1903), one of the more powerful and solitary contemporary writers, who lives far from Paris in the seclusion of Mount Desert Island, comes from an old aristocratic family, as did also Malraux' friend, Louise de Vilmorin (1902–1969).

But a selection of names is perforce arbitrary; hundreds of women are writing. They represent roughly three generations: those who, like Yourcenar and Beauvoir, were born before World War I; the generation of the twenties, whose early maturity coincided with World War II, a precocious generation; and the post-World War II generation, enmeshed in the particularly disconcerting French world of the sixties and seventies, uncertainly poised between a past it rejects and a future hard to imagine even in its immediacy. There seems no doubt at all that World War II awakened French women as a whole to a new sense of the inadequacy of the male governance of the world, just as the student rebellion in 1968, temporarily perhaps, stunned a group of young bourgeois women students who were much like the Americans the writer

Cynthia Ozick encountered when she gave a course in creative writing and whom she eloquently described.[7] The young women, like their male counterparts, she felt, passively, in fact, complacently, accepted current myths concerning woman's biological destiny and intellectual limitations. This traditional attitude was considerably strengthened by a belated upsurge of Freudian influence. Cynthia Ozick was outraged by the young Americans: "You could not tell the young men's papers from the young women's papers. They thought alike (badly), they wrote alike (gracelessly), and they believed alike (docilely). And what they all believed was this: that the minds of men and women are spectacularly unlike" (p. 433), the male's being by far the more interesting. The age-old prejudice often still holds, despite the absolute denial by such eminent scientists as Piaget that there are any discernable differences between the way a man's mind works and a woman's.

A vigorous postwar movement in favor of the emancipation of women has existed in France since World War II. But it has drawn only some five thousand participants. It perhaps reached its climax in November, 1970, when three hundred women from all walks of life convened in a three-day "States General of Women." That name itself, recalling the great days of the French Revolution, underscored these women's determination to be heard in matters of social and political debate, to participate in the shaping of policies, and to secure the recognition of women's independent and equal status. Women writers, although not all of them, have on the whole—like Simone de Beauvoir, Nathalie Sarraute, Marguerite Duras and Christiane Rochefort—been involved in the movement, lending their support and prestige to such causes as the repeal of the abortion laws, which concern all women.

When we turn to the field of criticism, a manifest contradiction exists: women writers have appeared in ever-greater number and received considerable attention from whatever reading public they reach. Obviously a poet like Edith Boissonnas, whom I cited in the first chapter, will not have the audience of a novelist like Christiane Rochefort. Neither do her male counterparts; poets, men or women, have the same kind of restricted audience. When the work of selection and historical ordering begins, however, a curious phenomenon occurs: there is a startling discrepancy between the number of women mentioned in any literary genre and the number of men. Several such works have recently appeared, attempting in a traditional way to bring order out of the chaos of today's literary productions. It is they who lay the groundwork for the establishment of a literary tradition. They are quite innocently, one feels, unaware of the fact that they are biased. But they most obviously are: one can almost follow the process step by step as, from repertory to critical survey, the names of women writers disappear, until, as in a history of *French Literature since 1945*,[8] the names of only eight French women are included, along with those of Virginia Woolf and three Canadian women writers; there are passing references to three or four others, who are critics, or mentioned, like Colette, as predecessors. Not a single woman poet is mentioned. This contrasts with the more than three hundred and fifty men cited— clearly an inflationary estimate. Without doubt, the women included are outstanding: Simone de Beauvoir, Simone Weil, Marguerite Yourcenar, Marguerite Duras, Nathalie Sarraute, and one who is possibly less significant, Françoise Sagan. But one could easily estimate that for two hundred out of the three hundred and fifty men cited, women as distinguished could be found. True, as the years go by, out of the three hundred and fifty names inscribed, few will survive; and finally perhaps a few centuries later, three or four women will stand out among a dozen men as truly great figures. This is what has happened in the late medieval and Renaissance volumes of the new history of French literature now being published by Arthaud.[9] But for the women writing in the present that is rather cold comfort. We witness here directly a literary tradition in the making. In spite of the present changes in the French woman's position, the critical tradition is obviously unfavorable to women writers.

In December of 1972, at the annual meeting of the American Association for the Advancement of Science, Dr. Elizabeth Tidball, who is a professor of physiology, presented a paper on the probability of career success for women undergraduates, based on the study of the careers of 1,100 women college graduates.[10] Her findings are clear. The higher the ratio of women faculty to women students, the greater the subsequent success of women students. In a coeducational situation the higher the percentage of men students enrolled in relation to women, the smaller the percentage of women "achievers" in subsequent careers. What seems clearly indicated, as Dr. Tidball stresses, is that for the young woman student, during the years when she must develop a firm identity and direct her energies toward the future, a cross-pressure develops, a conflict "between being an accomplished person and being a female." Here the presence of women who are prominent or merely competent weighs heavily, apparently, in the balance as a factor in the development of the young woman's confidence in her future.

The same may hold true in literature. Historians of literature up to now have been male academics who have inherited the old attitudes of the medieval clerics toward feminine achievement. They create their own models of "great writers" and tend to pay scant attention to the women. For the French woman who has overcome the social barriers and prejudices concerning her "nature," as well as the "image" held out to her by men, there is still, if she wants to write, the haunting spectre of failure. It haunts all artists, to be sure, but how much more deeply is the woman writer its prey? It haunts the pages of Simone de Beauvoir's memoirs as she painstakingly parries criticism by herself pointing out the shortcomings of her work. It is present in Colette, who describes one of her pseudo-selves, the heroine of *The Vagabond*, gazing in the mirror in a moment of discouragement at the face of *une femme de lettres ratée*, a woman writer who has come to nothing. The antidote for Colette was close at hand: it was the memory of Sido:

> Whenever I feel myself inferior to everything about me, threatened by my own mediocrity, frightened by the discovery that a muscle is losing its strength, a desire its power or a pain the keen edge of its bite, I can still hold up my head and say to myself: "I am the daughter of a woman who in a mean, close-fisted, confined little place opened her village home to stray cats, tramps and pregnant servant girls. . . . Let me not forget that I am the daughter of a woman who [when she was well past seventy] bent her head trembling, between the blades of a cactus, her wrinkled face full of ecstasy over the promise of a flower." [11]

It is interesting to see how, from woman writer to woman writer, signs of recognition are given: Louise Labé knows of Marguerite de Navarre, as Marie de Gournay knows of Christine de Pisan, as in our time Nathalie Sarraute speaks of Virginia Woolf and Ivy Compton Burnett, and Simone de Beauvoir of Colette and Ninon de Lenclos. In contrast to the wealth of male examples of success, there is a paucity of female mentors to whom women writers over the centuries may be compared: for women poets, "Sappho"; for scholars, "Minerva" or

"Hypatia." But a solid international tradition of feminist writing is now established, and its literary past is emerging more clearly every day. I think it is quite likely that the increasing number of women writers is a favorable sign, that it will encourage others.

Perhaps we shall have for some time still to speak of *women* writers, or, like Mr. Béalu, to present anthologies of *women* poets, in spite of the rightful impatience of these writers themselves. But as we have seen, the whole conception of literature is being re-examined in France in ways that may eventually work to the benefit of the woman writer. The very concept of "great genius," which *ipso facto* was applied negatively to women, is no longer operative today. Recently younger critics—both male and female—have started to explore literary structures in new ways. One of them, Tom Conley, notes that our recent awareness of feminist literature "has particular value in French prose where literary structures can be discerned, where in late medieval society, sources of creative energy can be pinpointed. One task—the beginning of a greater project—is to examine a number of formal modes in novels written by women; to dissect them; to situate where the tensions inherent in feminist writings are conjoined to an exterior social situation." [12]

He analyzes an early sixteenth-century novel in this light, *The Painful Anxieties Which Come from Love,* written by a woman, Hélisenne de Crenne, and usually considered as the first example of feminist "autobiography," with Hélisenne purportedly pouring out her heart in barely disguised fiction. He discovers a curious connection between the complex narrative structures of the novel and what he describes as "a constrictive sociological condition germinal to the creation of the feminist novel," "feminist" being used here as I have used it, meaning simply "written by a woman author." "Each aspect involves writing in cramped quarters and in moments of brief duration. Notes are taken in a room continually inspected by a jealous husband . . . a vicarious existence is attained via writing itself; the implied author creates letters and novels in which she finally becomes master of a given universe. All composition seems to take place in a closed room to which the harried protagonist retreats for solace and equilibrium" (p. 7). He recalls Virginia Woolf's approach to the art of the feminist novel in her essay *A Room of One's Own;* the evocation of the conditions in which Jane Austen, like so many other women, wrote: constrained, denied privacy, her range of experience limited (whereas men, it should be noted, have always had the prerogative to withdraw or be social at will). And he concludes as follows: "confession, letter-writing, self-conscious narrative romance . . . the indistinct passage from fact to fiction, complex psychological patterns: these all grew quite naturally from an absence of a 'room of one's own.' Hélisenne's *Angoysses* and the conditions of its creation suggest the advent of great novels in a unique and fecund tradition" (p. 7).

We are far from the question of the "nature of the feminine mind," exploring instead the processes and function of writing itself as it pertains to the particular situation of the person who writes. This approach gives us a clearer idea of how we may treat the question of the art of the woman writer in a way more pertinent than considering it automatically as a direct expression of an emotional experience—as French critics in the past have tended to do—because it offers structures that differ from prevalent forms. It is more interesting, for example, to see how, with little access to the literary milieu, to the prevailing conventions and fashions of the day, Hélisenne de Crenne emerged as a writer than to evaluate her, to her detriment, in terms of the "great" Balzac.

When in March, 1956, a review, *La Table Ronde,* made a survey of the conditions under which contemporary women writers work, it was rather startling to find that, after four centuries, many married women writers were still wrestling with the same difficult conditions as Hélisenne's, though for different reasons. This may perhaps explain the quite large number of single or divorced women writers, except where wealth creates that "locked door" between the writer and the world which Virginia Woolf called for. This, of course, may not change.

It would be dangerous to conclude from the few examples I have put before you that one can establish some kind of stereotype. But as opposed to the fond male image of her, there do seem to be certain recognizable personal characteristics that distinguish French women writers. Though less clear, situational traits too are shared by those writers whose careers I have so briefly sketched: the fierce dedication to some goal beyond themselves, the acceptance of infinitely hard and exhausting work, the willingness to transcend society's dictates. In all fairness, it should be noted that eventually, to the women thus committed, society ends by giving recognition, but it is understandable that few are willing to face the difficulties and the uncertainty in a realm where the chances of success tend to be pre-empted by men. Women *can* write today without the onus of having to compete with Shakespeare and Dante, Racine or Balzac. It was—and still is, though to a lesser extent—a perilous gamble; and success is available only to a few. To write, one must know something of the conditions in which literature is produced and be familiar with its exigencies as a craft; one must have access to an audience—court, salon, literary group—which, it would seem, must be aware of and interested in the vital intellectual issues of the period, those which impinge on the modes of sensitivity of the community.

These are preconditions which have not been of easy access to women nor particularly adapted to their social roles. Perhaps, in France, the greatest obstacle in their path has been strong persistence of the courtly tradition of love, degenerating into a mystique of woman as an *objet d'art*. Combined with the conception of the family embedded in the Napoleonic civil code, interiorized and taken as "natural," this image has weighed more heavily on French women's view of themselves than the commonly accepted Freudian one. It has affected their writing more deeply. Until recently it has been of necessity French women of the leisured class who have furnished the main contingent of women writers, particularly novelists, and there has of necessity been a conflict between the accepted role of the "woman of the world" with up-to-date cultural horizons, grace and wit, and the stringencies and hard work of writing. The role of Paris as the gathering center for the literati and dispenser of literary reputation has not always been particularly conducive, either for men or for women, to the development of seriously independent literary writing. There are too many short-cuts to a temporary recognition which, for women especially, once the novelty passes, soon fades. It takes a strong personality of independent means, like Marguerite Yourcenar, to develop as a writer far from Paris, its fads and conformisms. But almost always, in the past, some factor in the education of the women writers I have been examining has allowed them to escape the imposed social mold and thus facilitated the development of a personal point of view, so compensating for the lack of the broader experience and mobility of men, which women are only now beginning to enjoy.

It is a fact too that a great number of French women writers tend toward oversubjective, quasi-confessional types of novels. "The troupe [of women] continues to follow the direction, not of creative imagination, but of sensation, not of the setting up of characters or social milieux, but of personal confession," wrote Chonez in 1956.[13] Though several women have tried the path of the "new" experimental writing, her remark holds true even now. Writing for many seems the way to new personal independence or self-exploration rather than to literary achievement. And, as in the case of Violette Leduc, the desire to say everything that pertains to their life seems to be a way of breaking through the social taboos that have surrounded women's sensual life. Women writers of late have tended to be "image-breakers," depicting women within their novels without charity, battling perhaps against the masks or mythologies men have devised for them.[14] Nonetheless, because French women writers are in the thick of things today, the tendency is to classify them with literary groups, not in a group by themselves: Beauvoir is associated with the postwar literature of commitment, Duras and Sarraute with the new novel, Kristeva and Cixous with the experimental groups *Tel Quel* and *Poétique,* respectively. This is encouraging.

The general situation allows us, I think, to conclude that after more than five centuries, Christine de Pisan's characteristically reasonable prediction has at last been fully realized I shall quote from an old translation of her *Book of the City of Ladies,* in which she was answering that

tiresome old argument that women of accomplishment
are few:

> I say to thee again and doubt never the contrary that if it
> were custom to put the little maidens to school and they
> were made to learn the sciences as they do to the men-
> children, that they should learn as perfectly and they should
> be as well entered into the subleties of all the arts and
> sciences as men be. And peradventure there should be more
> of them.[15]

There are indeed more of them, and the way seems to be
opening toward a better and faster literary recognition.
But, ironically, French culture itself is now undergoing a
crisis which strikes at the root of the literary enterprise,
and the very abundance of women writing tends to sub-
merge them once again in the mass. It is difficult, then, to
foresee what the future holds. If it can reasonably be
assumed that French women will participate in all the
realms of their country's cultural activities in increasing
numbers and with greater self-assurance, the situation of
the woman writer will still remain problematic within a
culture in a process of transition.

It is perhaps fitting, then, to end on a note of caution.
As the century draws toward its end, literary women, like
literary men in France, seem uncertain of the future of
their art, and it may be some years before new, vigorous
currents of literary expression develop which would facili-
tate the appearance of substantial literary works. We

know little enough about the intricate connections that link artistic expression to the state of a society. But the accomplishment of French women writers in the last half-century seems to indicate that there is no lack of vitality or creative talent among them, if the circumstances prove favorable to its development.

NOTES

(All translations of quotations from French-language editions of works cited in this book are my own, unless otherwise noted).

PREFACE

[1] Georges Charbonnier, *Conversations with Claude Lévi-Strauss*, trans. John and Doreen Weightmen (London: Grossman, 1971), pp. 29–31.

CHAPTER ONE

[1] Marcel Béalu, *Anthologie de la poésie feminine française de 1900 à nos jours* (Paris: Stock, 195ȝ). Since then, there have been others, notably the two-volume anthology by Jeanne Moulin, *La Poésie féminine* (Paris: Pierre Seghers, 1963).

[2] Jean Rousselot, *Panorama critique des nouveaux poètes français* (Paris: Pierre Seghers, 1952).

[3] Virginia Woolf, *A Room of One's Own* (New York: Harcourt-Brace, 1929), p. 152.

[4] The definitions in the French Littré are even more revealing: "*Female*, animal of feminine sex: the female of the monkey. . . Used currently when speaking disparagingly of women." "*Male*, he who belongs to the sex physiologically characterized by the presence of the fecundating principle . . . a vigorous man, physically and morally." "*Feminine*, belonging to the sex physi-

ologically characterized by the ovary in animals and plants.
Distinctively characteristic of women." The first example given
is "considering the defects of the feminine creature." The Littré
does not list the words *féminisme* or *féministe*. More modern, the
Petit Robert dictionary gives only their political connotations.
Dictionaries are revealing; for the Littré, "female" or "feminine"
clearly suggests the connection with the animal or vegetable
kingdom, while "male" introduces quite different notions of
fecundity and nobility, while the link with the animal world is
elided. The medieval patterns are strongly embedded in the
definitions proffered.

⁵ Francis Jeanson, *Lettre ouverte aux femmes* (Paris: Editions
du Seuil, 1965); Françoise Parturier, *Lettre ouverte aux hommes*
(Paris: Albin Michel, 1968); Suzanne Lilar, *Le Malentendu du
deuxième sexe* (Paris: Presses Universitaires de France, 1972).
Lilar sensibly accepts the biological differences between the sexes
and some of their consequences and draws her argument from
certain biological facts. She points out that men and women
belong, in the first place, to the same species and furthermore
that only one out of the twenty-three pairs of genes that pro-
gram human development determines an individual's sexual
characteristics. Thence the large overlapping area of potentiali-
ties that the two sexes share. She accepts the psychological ob-
servations of Jean Piaget on the nondifferentiated mechanisms of
development of human intelligence, which reverse the medieval
concept of "reason" as the prerogative of men. Jeanson made
much of the physiological roles of men and women in the sexual
act, claiming superiority for the male role. This inspired Rabelai-
sian anger in Parturier, who attacked him for enshrining superiority in those few inches of flesh and bade him "put it back"
where it belonged and discuss the problem rationally. Her main
target was the condescending attitude of the Frenchman who

refuses to talk to women as adults and for whom any feminine problems can be solved by a little love-making.

[6] Marie José Chombart de Lauwe, *La Femme dans la société: son image dans les différents milieux sociaux* (Paris: C.N.R.S., 1963).

[7] Jean Larnac, *Histoire de la littérature féminine en France* (Paris: Editions Kra, 1929).

[8] Linda Nochlin, "Why Are There No Women Painters?", *Art News*, 69 (January 1971), 23–24; 67–69. Reprinted in Vivian Gornick and Barbara K. Moran, eds., *Woman in Sexist Society* (New York: Signet, 1972).

[9] Gustave Lanson, *Histoire de la littérature française*, 12e ed. (Paris: Hachette, 1912), p. 167.

[10] Françoise du Castel, *Damoiselle Christine de Pizan: veuve de Me Etienne de Castel, 1364–1431* (Paris: Editions A. et J. Picard, 1972), p. 94.

[11] Daniel Poirion, *Le Moyen Age II, 1300–1480*, Collection Littérature française, 2 (Paris: Arthaud, 1971).

[12] Françoise du Castel, *Damoiselle Christine*, p. 29. Subsequent quotations from Christine de Pisan are all drawn from this work and will therefore merely be referenced in the text. For the sake of convenience, I shall follow this practice with other authors.

[13] It has become customary today to refer to an older version of the Creation presented in *Genesis* 1:26–28, according to which men and women were created together: "So God created man in his own image, in the image of God he created him; male and female he created them," as opposed to the other, more familiar version in *Genesis* 2:18–24.

[14] Poirion, *Le Moyen Age*, p. 206.

[15] Françoise du Castel, *Damoiselle Christine*, p. 90.

[16] Yves Girard and Marc-René Jung, *La Renaissance I, 1480–*

1548, Collection Littérature française, 3 (Paris: Arthaud, 1972), p. 242.

[17] Louise Labé, *Oeuvres poétiques de Louise Labbé* (Paris: Le Club Français du Meilleur Livre, 1967), pp. 9–17.

[18] I have drawn my information from Marjorie Ilseley's authoritative book, *A Daughter of the Renaissance: Marie le Jars de Gournay* (The Hague: Mouton and Company, 1963). All quotations of Marie de Gournay's are from Ilseley, and the translations are hers.

CHAPTER TWO

[1] Guy de Maupassant, "Preface" to Abbé Prévost, *History of Manon Lescaut and of Le Chevalier des Grieux* (New York: Brentano, n.d.), pp. ix–xvi.

[2] Marie de Gournay, "Egalité des hommes et des femmes," in Marco Schiff, *La Fille d'alliance de Montaigne, Marie de Gournay* (Paris: Librairie Champion, 1910), p. 65.

[3] Simone de Beauvoir, *The Second Sex,* trans. H. M. Parshley (New York: Bantam Books, 1961), p. 535.

[4] The life at court centered upon Louis XIV, and, though women played a prominent role in the court rituals and intrigues, they lost a good deal of the independence they had shown in the early years of the century.

[5] After her husband's death, Madame de Sévigné did not remarry; Madame de Lafayette left her husband on his provincial estates and lived in Paris.

[6] The quotation, from *De l'Esprit des lois,* is cited in Leon Abensour, *La Femme et le féminisme avant la Révolution* (Paris: E. Lerous, 1923), p. 69.

[7] Antoine Caritat de Condorcet, "Sur l'admission des femmes au droit de cité," *Oeuvres,* X (Stuttgart-Bad Cannstatt: Frieduc Fromann Verlag, 1968), 119.

[8] Although an aristocrat by birth, George Sand's practicality seems better qualified by the term "bourgeois."

[9] Roger Shattuck, *The Banquet Years: The Arts in France, 1895–1918* (New York: Harcourt, Brace, 1958).

[10] Claudine Chonez, "Hier, aujourd'hui, demain," *La Table Ronde*, 99 (March, 1956), 61.

[11] Simone de Beauvoir, *The Second Sex*, pp. 664–665.

[12] Chonez, "Hier, aujourd'hui, demain," p. 63.

[13] Colette, *Break of Day*, trans. Enid McLeod (New York: Farrar, Straus and Giroux, 1966), p. 18.

[14] Henri Peyre, "Contemporary Feminine Literature in France," *Yale French Studies*, 27 (Spring–Summer, 1961), 49.

[15] Colette, *L'Etoile vesper* in *Oeuvres complètes*, XIII (Paris: Le Fleuron, 1949–50), 303.

[16] Colette, *The Blue Lantern*, trans. Roger Senhouse (New York: Farrar, Straus and Giroux, 1966), pp. 8–9.

[17] Edith Kern, "Author or Authoress?" *Yale French Studies*. 27 (Spring–Summer, 1961), 5.

[18] Simone de Beauvoir, *Pyrrhus et Cinéas* (Paris: Gallimard, 1944), p. 112.

CHAPTER THREE

[1] Elaine Marks, *Simone de Beauvoir: Encounters with Death* (New Brunswick: Rutgers University Press, 1973), p. 3.

[2] Simone de Beauvoir in *Que peut la littérature?* ed. Yves Brun, Collection l'Inédit (Paris: 10/18, 1965), p. 79.

[3] A university degree roughly equivalent to an M.A.

[4] In an interview published in *Contemporary Literature*, XIV, 2 (Spring, 1973), 137–146.

[5] Nathalie Sarraute, *Do You Hear Them?* trans. Maria Jolas, in *Fiction* I, 2 (Fall, 1972), 2.

[6] Renée Burkhardt, "Les Femmes ont perdu leur complexe de féminité," *La Table Ronde*, 99 (March, 1956), 95.

[7] Cynthia Ozick, "Woman and Creativity: The Demise of the Dancing Dog," in *Women in Sexist Society*, ed. Vivian Govniez and Barbara K. Moran (New York, 1972), pp. 431–451.

[8] J. Bersani, M. Autrand, J. Lecarme, and B. Vercier, *La Littérature française depuis 1945* (Paris: Bordas, 1970).

[9] Claude Pichois, ed., Littérature française, in 16 vols. (Paris: Arthaud, 1968–   ). The medieval period is covered by the first two volumes of the collection: Jean Charles Payen, *Le Moyen Age I, Des Origines à 1300* (1970); and Daniel Poirion, *Le Moyen Age II, 1300–1480* (1971). The Renaissance is being presented in the three subsequent volumes: Yves Girard and Marc-René Jung, *La Renaissance I, 1480–1548* (1972); Ena Balmas, *La Renaissance II, 1548–1570;* and Jean Morel, *La Renaissance III, 1570–1624.* (The last two volumes had not appeared as of the date of this book.)

[10] Dr. Elizabeth Tidball, "Perspective on Academic Women and Affirmative Action," published in abridged form in the *Educational Record* (Spring, 1973), 130–135.

[11] Colette, *Break of Day*, pp. 5–6.

[12] Tom Conley, "Feminism, *Ecriture* and the Closed Room: Hélisenne de Crenne's *Angoysses doulourseuses qui procedent d'amours* (1538)," unpublished Ms., University of Minnesota, p. 1.

[13] Chonez, "Hier, aujourd'hui, demain," p. 62.

[14] Virginia Anne Lipton, "Women in Today's World: A Study of Five French Women Novelists," unpublished dissertation, University of Wisconsin, 1972.

[15] Christine de Pisan, *Book of the City of Ladies*, in Blanche Hinman Dow, *The Varying Attitudes toward Women in French Literature of the Fifteenth Century* (New York: Institute of French Studies, 1936), p. 249.

DATE DUE
